# SPECIAL OPS

## JOURNAL OF THE ELITE FORCES

### & SWAT UNITS
### VOL.32

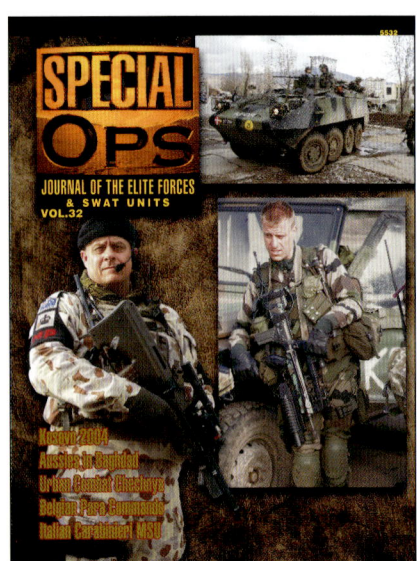

Editor: James R. Hill
Copyright © 2004
by CONCORD PUBLICATIONS CO.
603-609 Castle Peak Road
Kong Nam Industrial Building
10/F, B1, Tsuen Wan
New Territories, Hong Kong
www.concord-publications.com

We welcome authors who can help expand our range of books. If you would like to submit material, please feel free to contact us.

We are always on the look-out for new, unpublished photos for this series. If you have photos or slides or information you feel may be useful to future volumes, please send them to us for possible future publication. Full photo credits will be given upon publication.

ISBN 962-361-099-8
printed in Hong Kong

# KOSOVO 2004

**Yves Debay**

## Multinational Brigade North East in the Eye of the Storm

A Pandur sits in front of a destroyed Serbian home. The Pandur has a crew of 2+8 for a combat weight of 14 tons. It has a range of 700 km (435 miles) and it has a maximum road speed of 100 km/h. Its basic armament is a 7.62mm or 12.7mm MG.

### The "Desert of Tartars" in a Garbage Dump

Buckling on their backpacks at the end of January 2004, the "White Bisons" of the *126ème Régiment d'Infanterie* (RI) [126th Infantry Regiment] have no doubt that they soon will be plunging into action. Among the various deployments made by the French land forces, Kosovo is not popular. It is the French Army's fifteenth mandate and a certain routine has set in over the years.

For the soldiers, the patrols in this infernal "Desert of Tartars" strewn with the garbage that is Mitrovica are far from motivating. It is with a certain amount of jealousy that the soldiers of the 4th Company and the Support Company of the *126ème Régiment d'Infanterie* see their companions in other companies leaving France for Ivory Coast. But a soldier's duty is to obey, and so the regiment is supplying two companies, one of which is the famous CRO (*Compagnie de réserve opérationelle* [Operational Reserve Company]) to BATFRA (*bataillon français* [French Battalion]) of the MNB-North East in Kosovo. The commanding officer,

Soldiers of the CEA (Compagnie d'éclairage et d'appui – Reconnaissance and Support Company) of the 126ème Régiment d'Infanterie (RI) (126th Infantry Regiment) prepare to go out on patrol in the southern part of Mitrovica.

Prior to going out on patrol, the soldiers of the CEA of the 126th receive a short briefing from the NCO in command of the groupe de combat (combat group (squad)). The strange cage on the VAB that is covered with a camouflage net is used to store the riot shield, which can be fitted inside the narrow combat compartment of the vehicle.

Troops await the order to stand guard at the bridge. The stance of the corporal on the right is typical of troops wearing a flak jacket; the positioning of the hand relieves pressure on the shoulders.

- A command and support battalion (France);
- The BATFRA (under French command but with various foreign units);
- The DANBAT (under Danish command with the French EEI-3 [*Escadron d'éclarage et d'investigation* – Reconnaissance squadron] in VBL light armored vehicles); and
- The Greek 507th Mechanized Battalion, which operates in the Brigade's zone but has a special status and is tasked with watching the Pristina-Mitrovica axis. (This "battalion" consists of only one combat company.)

Infantrymen of the CEA of the 126ème RI. Their uniform and equipment are characteristic of the French infantry at the beginning of the 21st century: Spectra helmet (which is worn only on wartime missions) and the flak jacket. The flak jacket is heavy but performs well in combat. (This was proven during the assault on the Vrbanja Bridge in Sarajevo where each of the attacking French soldiers was hit but not wounded.) The little red wire over the left shoulder is used to quickly open the flak jacket in case the soldier is wounded.

General Michel, doubtless notices with a certain resentment the loss of power in the brigade. He only has a handful of helicopters at his disposal, and if he had to he could scrape up about 3000 men. It is at the same time too many men and not many men in case of a problem, and the facts would quickly confirm it. At the command post in Novo Cello on the Pristina road, the table of effectives for the Brigade lists the following forces:

This groupe de combat has debussed from its VAB to relieve their comrades at the southern entrance of the Mitrovica bridge in the Albanian sector.

A soldier of the 126th RI patrols with a dog in southern Mitrovica. Dog handlers in the French Army are detached for four months to serve in a regiment on duty in an operational theatre.

*A view from the north (which is the Serbian side) of a VAB of the 126ème RI at the entrance to the "Austerlitz" bridge. The 126th, which belongs to the 3ème Brigade Mécanisée (3rd Mechanized Brigade), assumed the main operation during the crazy and tense week chronicled in this article. Twelve soldiers of the regiment were wounded, two very badly.*

*VAB armored vehicle of the 126ème RI seen on the "Austerlitz" bridge in Mitrovica, which became a symbol separating the Albanians in the south from the Serbs in the north.*

Basically, General Michel articulated the operation as follows: the BATFRA keeps watch over Mitrovica, the border with Serbia and certain enclaves. The DANBAT patrols all of the west and the southwest region of the Brigade's AOR (area of responsibility).

We should not fail to mention the presence of the men and women of the Moroccan military hospital, who will play more than a positive role in the events, though they were not prepared for it. The Moroccans, under the patronage of the Princess Lala Myriam, have established a magnificent hospital that doubles as a social assistance program that benefits the local populations.

Those who in theory do not make war but are charged with avoiding it, even through the use of weapons, are the soldiers of the BATFRA and the DANBAT.

## A Streamlined Operation

The first operation included 1298 soldiers and consisted of:
- a staff from the 1/11 *Cuirassiers* (heavy cavalry)
- UCL (*Unité de commandement et logistique* – Command and Logistic Unit) of the 1/11
- the 4th Company of the *126ème Régiment d'Infanterie*
- the CEA (*Compagnie d'éclairage et d'appui* – Recce and Support Company) of the *126ème* RI
- the road traffic squadron of the *517ème Régiment de Train* (Transport Regiment)
- three light *Proterre* companies composed of two sections
- one Moroccan motorized company
- one Belgian paratrooper company of the Belgian 3rd Paras, with a recce platoon from Luxembourg.

*Note the "white bison" insignia on the front of this VAB. The symbol was used in World War One when the "126" was a famous fighting unit.*

A sniper of the 126ème RI is in the position where they were forced to reply and kill three Albanian snipers entrenched in the "three towers" when they opened fire on French troops. The rifle in use is the 7.62mm FR-F2. Note the map and photographs of areas that could likely be used by hostile elements. Note also the small hill on the northern (Serbian) side that dominates Mitrovica and has a strange monument on it (a tribute to the mining industry) that the soldiers call "the barbecue."

A French sniper with a Hecate PGM 12.7mm-caliber heavy sniping rifle. The French Army made a difference with their tireurs de précision (sharpshooters) armed with FR-F2 rifles in each squad (four per company) and the snipers operating a small team of two FR-F2s and a 12.7mm PGM mounted on a VAB that is fitted with a 20mm gun. They are under the direct command of a company commander, usually a captain, and are used to suppress enemy snipers, as was done in Mitrovica last March and several times in Sarajevo.

A VAB of a Proterre company. The Proterre is a light marching company made up of two sections that are mounted only for overseas deployment. The VAB seen here was used by various units, as is shown by the badge, a Moroccan green star, and the red devil of the 152ème RI, which is the other infantry regiment in the 3rd Mechanized Brigade.

The Danes of the DANBAT know Mitrovica very well. The unit numbers 500 men who are divided up among a command and logistic company, a large infantry company composed of three sections from the Danish Life Guard (mounted on M113A6s) and two platoons from the Jutland Dragoons (riding Mowag Piranha IIIs), a Latvian recce squadron (on Mercedes Wolf 4x4s), and an EEI recce squadron in VBLs supplied by the 1/11 Cuirassiers.

General Michel can really only count on approximately 1500 people.

### Mitrovica: A Place Made for Confrontation

To understand the series of events in Mitrovica, a short study of the geography of the Brigade's AOR is necessary. The Brigade holds northern Kosovo and the only city where a certain balance exists among the Albanians and the Serbs: Mitrovica. The Ibar river flows there from east to west, separating the north (which is populated mostly by Serbs) from southern Albania. In theory, bridges unite people, but in Mitrovica they are the stakes in a relentless struggle. The principal bridge is "Austerlitz." Farther to the east is "Cambronne," which is strictly controlled by KFOR

and flanked with military posts covered in sandbags, such as "Zelda" on the Serb side. Two large buildings flank the southern part of "Austerlitz": the headquarters of the Operational Reserve Company of the 126ème RI in charge of holding the bridge and, on the other side, the headquarters of UNMIK.

The problem is that there is an Albanian settlement situated in the north that has become a symbol: the "Three Towers" complex on the north bank of the Ibar, which is a real provocation for the Serbs and a bridgehead into hostile territory for the Albanians. A small footbridge was built to allow the inhabitants to shop on the Albanian south bank of the Ibar. Naturally, the place is permanently guarded by at least two platoons. Every Sunday, the Serbs can pass to the south under strong escort on their way to Mass at the church of Saint Avant.

If the Albanians have their ghetto north of the Ibar, farther south along the north-south flow and along the Pristina-Mitrovica railway spreads out the majority of the totally isolated Serbian enclaves, two of the most important being Grade and Preludje. A Serbian leaving the area without a military escort is practically courting death. The picture would not be complete without mentioning the presence of orthodox convents – Benja, Slatina and Device – which are isolated in UCK territory and guarded by small KFOR detachments.

### Demonstration Turns into Revolt

The Brigade was put on alert on Tuesday, March 16 at 1830 hours. UNMIKPOL has asked the MNB-NE to help to find two missing children from Cabra. DANBAT leads the search along the Ibar with the help of two American Blackhawk helicopters equipped with searchlights. One body is found near the village of Cabra by the KPC (Kosovo Protection Corps), an Albanian paramilitary unit that is officially recognized and which contains a number of former members of the UCK. The second body was found near the village on the 17th at 0630 in the morning.

On the morning of the 17th, inflamed by comments on the television, thousands of Albanians converge, heading toward Mitrovica for a peaceful demonstration. It begins calmly enough with a procession of children silently walking past the bridge, which is guarded by an anti-riot unit of UNMIK (United Nations Mission Kosovo) consisting of Pakistanis and Jordanians. The CRO of the 4ème Compagnie of the 126ème RI is naturally on the alert.

Hardly has the procession of children passed by when hundreds of Albanians assault the "Austerlitz" bridge. Three 4x4s of the UNMIK are quickly set ablaze while stones, bolts and Molotov cocktails rain down on

VBL of the EEI-3 (Escadron d'éclairage et d'investigation), which is the recce unit of the 3ème Brigade Mécaniseé attached to the tank regiment of the 1/11 Cuirassiers. The VBLs are being used to mount a hastily deployed mobile checkpoint, which is the best way to stop and arrest armed people in a country like Kosovo. Due to the use of mobile phones, a mobile checkpoint is only effective for about 20 minutes.

the bridge. Assisted by soldiers of the "126", the policemen hold their position. They have placed their 6x6 armored vehicles wheel to wheel to block the bridge.

The fight began at 1100 in the morning and lasted for two hours, but the rioters were unable to get by. UNMIK evacuated the building during the panic, and the "white bisons" took immediate possession of it so the rioters could not burn it down. (The Albanian extremists are considered to

be practically at war with the UNMIK. On the 21st, masked men in camouflage dress shot down two Ghanian policemen.)

At the other bridge, "Cambronne", Belgian para-commandos under the command of Captain Defranq expect to be attacked at any time. The garrison at the bridge consists of only two paratroops platoons and the command platoon of the 17th Company of the Belgian 3rd Para. Two other platoons were sent to reinforce the "Austerlitz" bridge.

The VBL squadron is composed of a command and logistics platoon, a technical information platoon equipped with a RASIT radar group on VABs, and three recce platoons. The recce platoons contain a command patrol with two VBLs (CP version) and three patrols of two VBLs, each of which is fitted with different armaments (2x112mm Apilas rocket launchers, two Milan anti-tank missiles, and two 12.7mm MGs).

The traffic squadron (Escadron de circulation routière) of the 517ème Régiment du Train was not really prepared to intervene in a riot but they remained calm and protected some of the Serb enclaves such as Slatina. Note the impact of the stone on the bottom of the windscreen. The machine gun is a 7.62mm AFn.

The Belgian para-commandos of the 17th Company of the 3rd Para are elite soldiers. The Belgian para-commando brigade is famous throughout NATO, and General Michel was happy to have these "crack" troops on call during the recent events in Mitrovica.

The officer of the Belgian Red Berets also hears the outcry of the crowd outside the *Saint Avant* church located three hundred meters (328 yards) south of his position. Molotov cocktails explode against the religious site, which is being held by a platoon of Moroccan soldiers.

At midday, a large part of the crowd suddenly splits off along the Ibar and hurries around the footbridge leading to the "three towers." At 1300 hours they attack. The Danish platoon guarding the bridge fires all of its teargas grenades. They are only able to hold back the crowd for half an hour. At 1400 in the afternoon, more than one thousand furious Albanians cross the Ibar River, with others pushing on behind, and the thin Danish contingent is forced to retreat for its own survival. Afterward, an enormous crowd (some of them armed) races toward the towers. The Serbs, seeing KFOR overwhelmed, react. Soon gunfire can be heard. The Albanians respond, and Mitrovica echoes with bursts from Kalashnikovs.

General Michel has no more choice. The belligerents must be immediately separated otherwise the riot can become a street fight. Political consequences could be terrible. The *4ème Compagnie* of the *126ème* RI, part of the CEA and the Danish Life Guards intervene. After two hours of fighting, the "white bisons" of the 126th succeed in restoring order and repelling the Albanians on the other side of the Ibar. The soldiers repeatedly make use of their FAMAS assault rifles. The cost is heavy: four Albanians and two Serbs were killed and 250 were wounded, 12 of which are French and Danish.

Belgian paratroops patrol on the streets of Vucitirn, an Albanian city south of Mitrovica.

After a neutral zone is created, a night filled with danger settles on Mitrovica.

On the night of the 16/17, the Italian *carabinieri* anti-riot police of the MSU (Multinational Specialized Unit), which is the intervention reserve of the KFOR, arrives from Pristina and relieves the Belgian paratroopers at the "Cambronne" bridge. This means one less worry for General Michel because the Italian *carabinieri* are particularly well equipped and are motivated to face down the rioters. The newly freed Belgian detachment goes at once to patrol near the villages of Stari Trag and Trepeca, north of Mitrovica. The two Serb villages command the entrance into an Albanian valley. If the paratroops chase the Serbs from these two villages, they will

Like the rest of the light troops in the Western world, after the end of the Cold War, the Belgian paras were forced to adopt armored vehicles to protect themselves.

*The Belgian government bought 54 Austrian Pandur vehicles in 2000. Only one platoon of four was attached to the Belgian contingent in Kosovo.*

be able to get to Mitrovica from the east and thus create a new front and start to encircle the city.

At their arrival, the Belgian Red Berets notice that the Serbs are ready to defend themselves and that the fight had already begun, with Albanian snipers firing on the village. The presence of Belgian paras will immediately calm the game.

### Moroccans Evacuate a "Pope"

Throughout Kosovo, news is alarming. Hundreds of Serbs are chased from their burning homes and religious buildings. At Prizren, the barricades of the MINUK and the German soldiers are crushed, and the crowd sets fire to the cathedral, before going on to destroy a historic convent dating from the 13th century. In reprisal, mosques in Belgrade and Nis are destroyed.

*A "bridge too far" in Mitrovica. Here a Belgian paratrooper patrols a bridge in Vucitirn. Note the soldier's Accuracy International rifle, which the Belgians call their anti-terrorist counter-sniper rifle. One is in service in each section (combat group).*

*The Belgian company, which was attached to BATFRA in Mitrovica, was organized around the 17th Company of 3rd Para. It consists of a HQ, three infantry platoons and a Luxembourg recce platoon on Humvees. Normally they are in Kosovo for only four months, but due to the events of March, they were forced to stay for an extra two weeks.*

This Belgian para is armed with a 5.56mm FNC CAL assault rifle.

Each Belgian infantry platoon consists of 35 men: one officer, four NCOs and 30 paratroops. At the beginning of the troubles, a lone Belgian platoon was on the "Cambronne" bridge. It is a lucky thing that the Albanians did not try to force their way across because the Belgian troops would not have hesitated for one second to open fire.

On the morning of the 17th, the commotion of combat resounds at the Moroccan hospital. Rumors indicate that the crowd is going to assault the now-vacant Koufra barracks where the hospital is located, and which is guarded only by a handful of French soldiers from Headquarters. Some of the male nurses and doctors quickly don their flak jackets and helmets and pick up their FAL assault rifles before taking up improvised combat positions. A crowd estimated at 3000 hurries to the district. Their target is the *Saint Avant* church.

A Belgian paratrooper armed with a 5.56mm Minimi, which is currently the most famous Belgian weapon in the world. Two of them are in service in each section. Note the beret badge with the medieval axes and flail, which characterized the Flemish militia in the Middle Ages.

On the previous night, the Moroccan soldiers formed a human shield to evacuate the "pope" (Orthodox priest) by means of a hole in the outer wall that is adjoined to the district. Then, following a decision by Lieutenant Colonel Belfkih, the commander of the Morocco hospital, the religious leader was exfiltrated in the night by a French Puma helicopter. His church would not survive him.

In the morning, the crowd approaches. Twenty-five Moroccans facing several thousand demonstrators hold their position under an avalanche of stones and Molotov cocktails. For General Michel, the dilemma is simple: to avoid the burning of the church, the order must be given to open fire. But of course this is not possible without causing a slaughter. The Moroccans march off and the church burns.

In the rest of the zone, the two VBLs of the EEI-1/11 *Cuirassiers* cannot prevent the crowd from destroying the historic monastery at Device, whose nuns were already abused in 1999 and saved by the French and Norwegian Special Forces.

The Latvians, who guarded the monastery of Banja, were able to prevent its destruction. After the violence of the morning, a precarious peace reigns over Mitrovica. The soldiers can rest a bit. The operation is stabilized on all sensitive points.

At about 2030 hours, shots are fired from one of the "three towers" in the direction of the building where the men of the CRO reside. The Frenchmen, with all the calm of veteran troops, do not return fire, but give the alert to their sharpshooters who are in position in a neighboring building.

At 2110, new shooting is heard. A bullet passes within 30 centimeters

*Each section (combat group) consists of two Minimi, one MAG or 12.7mm mounted on the Pandur, one sniper rifle, and four FNC CAL. The driver is armed with a 9mm pistol. Each soldier can carry an M-72 LAW rocket launcher and 10 AFLA phosphorous rifle grenades. The soldiers also carry a phosphorous grenade and a HE grenade.*

(one foot) of the head of one soldier. This shot was fired from another tower. This time, with lives in danger, the commander does not hesitate for a second: fire is returned immediately. Four soldiers of the rifleman group of the CEA of the *126ème* RI squeeze the triggers on their FR-F2, and the two Albanian snipers "hidden" in the tower are shot down simultaneously with two bullets apiece.

### Airborne Reinforcements Arrive

The day before, Paris, seeing the gravity of the situation and in agreement with NATO headquarters and the NAC (National Atlantic Counci\l) decides to send reinforcements to the area. Some 3500 taken from the Alliance's strategic reserve leave for Kosovo. Among the first to arrive are French paratroops that demonstrate that they understand the urgent nature of the situation.

In this month of March, the *Guépard* alert is the responsibility of the *1er Régiment de Chasseurs Parachutistes* (RCP) [1st Regiment of *Chasseurs* Parachutists]. In theory, a regiment on *Guépard* alert has to supply a combat company in less than twelve hours, an EMT (*Etat-major tactique* - tactical staff) and one CEA (support company) in 48 hours, and a second combat company in under 48 hours. On 18 March, the first C-160 Transall takes off from Toulouse-Francazal at 1300 hours. Four others follow, bringing 350 eager parachutists, who are distributed among an EMT and two combat companies (HQ of the *1er* RCP, *1er* Coy, *1er* RCP and *4ème Coy, 3ème* RPIMa (*Régiment Parachutiste d'Infanterie de Marine* – Marine Infantry Parachute Regiment).

The arrival of the paras would be a relief to General Michel, who would be able to strengthen his operation. On the 19th, the "Leopards" of the *4/3ème* RPIMa go immediately to the relief of the Danish troops at the three towers, who conduct operations during the day in search of weapons.

(The Scandinavian troops are serious about their work, and any locked door is opened with explosives.) The *1er Compagnie* (1st Company) of the *1er* RCP increases the number of their patrols. New reinforcements arrive in the form of troops from the Belgian 1st *Lanciers*, who would normally relieve the 3rd Para. The Belgian Red Berets would nevertheless pursue their mission until the restoration of peace.

*Danish armor or vehicles in front of the "three towers." A crowd of Albanian rioters overran the position on 17 March after they crossed the Ibar River at the right in the photo via a small footbridge.*

*Guarded by Latvians, a Mowag Piranha III of the Jutland Dragoons crosses a bridge over the Ibar 10km (6.2 miles) south of Mitrovica. Note the barbed wire on the front of the vehicle.*

In Mitrovica, which the MNB-North East has perfectly locked up, the situation has stabilized. One final incident occurs near the "Austerlitz" bridge when a drunken Serb throws a handmade grenade at the soldiers guarding the bridge. The man is arrested by his own countrymen, who then hand him over to the MINUK police.

### The Failure of KFOR

Twenty-eight dead. Six hundred wounded, 61 of which belong to KFOR. Thousands of people displaced. Three hundred homes burned. Twenty-nine monasteries and churches destroyed. In four days, between

*Danish soldiers of the Danish Life Guard at the foot of one of the "three towers." One Danish soldier and 12 French infantrymen of the 126ème RI were wounded on the afternoon of 17 March. It was from this tower that Albanian snipers opened fire and were killed by retaliatory fire from French counter-sniping riflemen.*

*A Mowag Piranha III of the Jutland Dragoons. Two platoons from this famous regiment that is so familiar with the Balkans were involved in the action. Denmark has 22 Piramha IIIs. Note the small homemade cage that protects the machine gunner against thrown stones.*

*Danish Mercedes Wolf vehicles belonging to the Jutland Dragoons recce platoon. Note the large wire cutter fitted to the vehicle.*

16 and 20 March 2004, four years of effort in Kosovo were ruined, and an uncertain future settles over the province. Temporarily, the Albanian extremists conducted a successful if limited ethnic cleansing operation right under the eyes of a powerless KFOR, who never saw it coming.

A French officer, speaking anonymously, told us, "Generally, when the alarm signal is at red, the leaders of KFOR quickly anticipate events and control the source of violence. But this time we were totally surprised."

*Keeping watch in the cold. A young Latvian soldier smokes a cigarette while on guard duty.*

*An M113A2 that was used as a HQ sits in front of the small combat post at the foot of the "three towers." The M113 was upgraded for the Balkans operation with the ACAV shield for the 12.7mm MG, and the additional armor.*

Latvian reconnaissance troops guard a bridge spanning the Ibar River not far from the village of Cabra, where two children drowned. The incident was used as a pretext for Albanian rioting.

Greek soldiers are not attached to the MNB-North West but are tasked with protecting the main road to Kosovo, especially the north-south axis "Hawk", which is the main supply route from Skopje in Macedonia to Mitrovica via Pristina.

A company of the 507th Mechanized Battalion is seen here at a checkpoint south of Mitrovica.

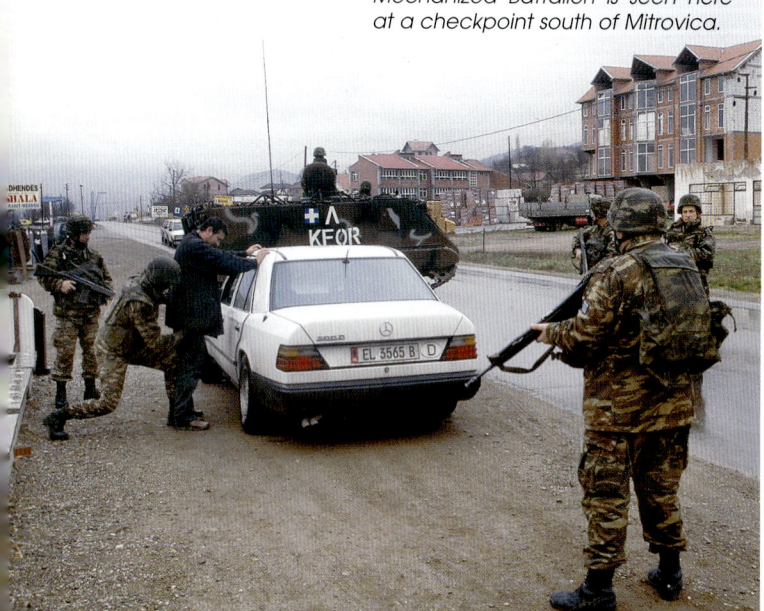

With the exception of the uniform, which is the U.S. woodland-pattern battle dress uniform, the Latvian equipment (Wolf vehicles, flak jackets, 7.62mm x 51 G-3 assault rifles) all comes from the Danish Army. Latvian and Lithuanian soldiers are often attached to Danish troops during peacekeeping missions.

In fact, the absence of reliable information on this eruption of violence and the lack of advanced warnings doubtless resulted from the decrease in means of intelligence and the routine into which KFOR had fallen. The NATO force in Kosovo had shrunk down from 40,000 men to 17,500 men over a two-year period. Only the American troops of the MNB-East (Multinational Brigade-East) still have heavy tanks.

To better understand the events discussed in this article, a brief review of the history of Kosovo is helpful.

During the rule of Tito, the Yugoslav President gave to Kosovo an autonomous status while still retaining it as a province in the Yugoslav Federation. Distrustful of Serbian nationalism, Tito wanted to reduce Serbian influence in a province where the demographic balance began to favor the Albanians [1]. The Serbs consider Kosovo to be sacred ground. It was in Prizren that Stefan Ducan based the Serbian nation in the 13th century. Convents and churches flourished in the province. Three battles of *Kosovo Polje* (Field of Blackbirds) resulted in Serbia losing its independence to the Ottoman invaders, who would stay in the Balkans for five centuries.

(1)     Before World War Two, the demographic balance among the Serbs and Albanians was well balanced. Figures reported about 200,000 souls in a province about the size of Brittany. Some 50,000 Serbs were chased from their homes by Albanian fascist militia supported by the Nazis.
In the 1950s and 1960s, thousands of Albanian refugees fleeing the communist dictatorship of Enver Hodja were welcomed into the province with benevolence by the Tito regime. This new contribution would upset the demographic balance of Kosovo. The newcomers (who professed the Moslem religion) had a reproductive rate superior to the Serbian population. The Albanian population has increased from 250,000 in 1948 to an estimated 1,500,000 today. There are 80,000 Serbs in the northern part of the country and 20,000 in enclaves. Some 280,000 persons (226,000 Serbs and 37,000 Rom) chased away from Kosovo now live in Serbia.

Forty years after its inception, the M113 armored personnel carrier is the most commonly seen armored vehicle in the world. These two Greek M113 are seen manning a checkpoint.

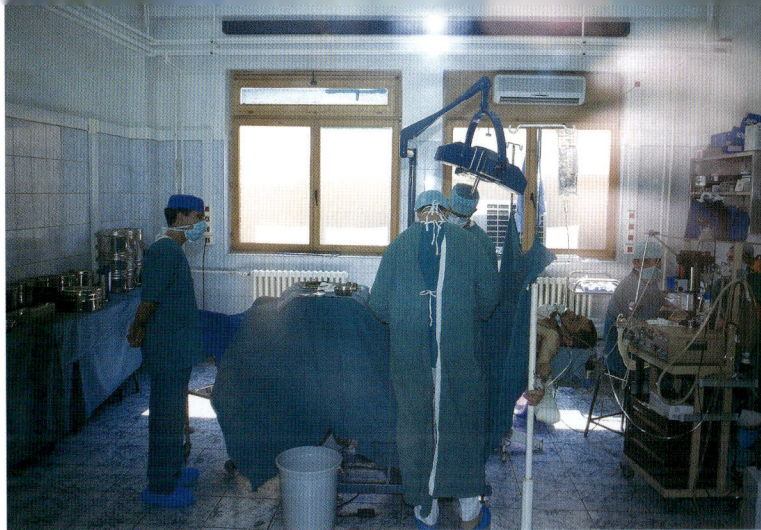

Moroccan medical personnel perform surgery at a hospital. The Moroccan hospital was set up in a former Yugoslav Army barracks called "Koufra" that was used for a long time as the French HQ in Mitrovica. After the French troops left, the Moroccan medical staff was isolated, but the personnel did not believe they would be involved in action during the eruption of violence in March.

During the implosion of Yugoslavia in the 1990s, Milosevic cancelled the autonomous status of the province of Kosovo. In reaction to this act, an Albanian resistance movement was created, and the UCK immediately began combat operations.

The Serbian army quickly occupied the province and began to fight the guerillas. A skillfully orchestrated press campaign made Serbia the target of criticism from other nations. Responding to charges of genocide and massacres, and seeing the influx of refugees, NATO (without the approval of the UN) began an air campaign against Serbia. Though NATO's fighter-bombers destroyed strategic targets, they could not break through the tactical anti-aircraft umbrella of the JA (Yugoslav Army) without suffering heavy losses.

In June of 1999, following negotiations, a still-intact Serbian Army left Kosovo and turned over the province to a multinational force under a UN mandate: KFOR. KFOR was tasked with protecting minorities, including Serbians, Rom (Gypsies), Bosnians, Croatians, Ashkili, and Turks. United Nations Resolution 1244 did not absolutely modify the status of the province, which remains officially a province of Serbia-Montenegro. Albanian Kosovars pay little attention to this and continue to dream of independence or of reunification with Albania.

The province, cut by Serbia and at the mercy of a Mecedonian blockade, is not economically viable. Three quarters of the population are unemployed, and the rest make a living on the trafficking that is common to wartime regions. Worse still, Kosovo is becoming the rearguard of the

Moroccan nurses and social workers hand out toys and clothing to the Rom (Gypsy) community. The Roms suffered prosecution at the hands of the Albanians.

This ACMAT 8x8 truck carries a medical shelter that belongs to the Moroccan hospital, which entered into service in 2000. Each shelter has its own mission.

The Humvee is the main light vehicle and liaison vehicle in use by the Moroccan contingent.

*The Royal Moroccan Army sent a combat company to be attached to BATFRA. The soldiers were transported by French Army VABs, which retained their French camouflage. In Morocco, the King's Army uses the 6x6 VAB.*

Albanian "mafias" in Europe. The Albanian "mafias", which are well entrenched on the continent and are often composed of former members of the UCK, reign over a hidden economy that is fed on drug dealing, prostitution, organ trafficking, and arms dealing. Some of this money is laundered in Kosovo hotels and service stations. (There are 30 service stations along the 38-kilometer [24-mile] road between Mitrovica and Pristina!)

One might wonder why the Albanians, who are well protected by KFOR, would wish to provoke trouble in the province. It is probably economic and political frustration manifesting itself through internal dissention. "In five years," says Alex Anderson of the ICG (International Crisis Group), "the question of Kosovo's final status has not advanced an inch." In the eyes of Albanian extremists, provoking an explosion of violence can only contribute to the mayhem and, at the same time, lead to an ethnic cleansing operation.

Two catalytic events set fire to the proverbial powder keg at the beginning of the spring of 2004. The first passed relatively unnoticed. On Monday, March 15, a Serb was murdered in Pristina. As a sign of protest, the Serbian community blocked the Pristina-Skopje road as far as Gracanica. In the eyes of the Albanians, KFOR intervened weakly. Soon

*Moroccan soldiers sit atop a VAB, using it as an effective observation post. In case of a skirmish, they will quickly disappear inside the vehicle to benefit from its armor protection. Note that the soldiers are wearing flak jackets.*

*Soldiers from Morocco patrol in Serbian enclaves. They are armed with the famous Belgian FN FAL 5.56mm assault rifle. Moroccan troops are generally strong, tough and courageous. Along with the Jordanians, they are considered to be the best Arab soldiers.*

*A Moroccan motorized company mounted on a VAB guards the Serbian enclave of Slatina. In both the First World War and the Italian campaign of 1944, the French soldiers appreciated the Moroccan troops. The Moroccan motorized company is composed of a command platoon and three platoons.*

*The older Moroccan soldiers have combat experience against Polisario in Western Sahara. Note their "lizard" camouflage, which is similar to that worn by the French during the war in Algeria.*

the first incident would take place between the Swedish soldiers and Albanian demonstrators who want to burn the convent situated near the road.

The next day, an incident took place that would be used as a pretext for violence. Under circumstances that remain unclear, three Albanian children drowned in the Ibar River near the village of Cabra, which is a sort of mini-Mitrovica, a village cut in two by two communities. A complaint was registered with UNMIK, but Albanian media and local politicians seized on the tragedy and exaggerated the facts. One child that was interviewed on television asserted that Serbs, with the help of dogs, pushed the children to the river. On Wednesday morning, the daily newspaper *Koha* asserted "Serbs Kill Three Albanian Children." Another daily paper, *Epoka*, twisted the words of the Serbian president, Vladimir Kostunica, by evoking his "appeal in the murder of the Albanians." This lack of objectivity by the local media, supported by a part of the political class, would provoke a series of "spontaneous" demonstrations that would degenerate into ethnic purification operations.

It seems that some of these events had been perfectly organized in advance far from this springtime violence. One indication of this is that buses crammed with students quickly headed out to Mitrovica. In the MND-South West sector (German-Italian), the Albanian extremists in Prizren attacked Serb homes in Belo-Polje south of Pec, while they are replaced locally by people (who are unknown to the military authorities) who attacked the monasteries of Recane.

*After the eruption of violence, the GCP of the 1er RCP (Régiment de Chasseurs Parachutistes) were quickly sent to the scene. Here they patrol the border region near Serbia, which is characterized by mountainous terrain. The KFOR command was upset by the Serbian reaction to the Albanian violence, and these patrols were organized to see if weapons were being smuggled through the area and sent to Serb enclaves.*

*A Mamba, a mineproof vehicle used by the UNMIK, is shown in front of the UN's HQ vehicles. Albanian rioters destroyed several UN vehicles on 16 March.*

*Each regiment of French paratroopers contains two teams of Pathfinders, free-fall specialists who compose what is called a GCP (Groupe Commando Parachutiste). The GCP of the four airborne infantry regiments could also be grouped together and work directly for the 11ème Brigade Parachutiste.*

After a patrol, the GCP poses for a souvenir photograph in front of a Peugeot P-4 vehicle. Note the different weapons: FAMAS and FR-F2 rifles. Normally, the GCP would also have an MP-5 submachine gun, but there is none present in this photo.

A GCP of the 1er RCP patrols in the mountains near the Serbian border. The para in the foreground is armed with a semi-automatic riot gun.

At Djakovica, a crowd of 2500 persons attacked the small orthodox convent that housed four aged nuns, the only Serbs in the village. Italian paratroops of the Folgore Brigade were forced to fire at the legs of the rioters to prevent them from lynching the nuns. The convent was left in ashes.

KFOR, surprised and totally overextended, was able to save some lives but was unable to prevent the destruction of houses and the death of 28 persons. A Serbian refugee declared to us, "Five centuries of Ottoman occupation: 200 churches and convents destroyed. Five years of NATO presence: 150 convents and churches destroyed."

Paradoxically, in the long term, the crisis can only strengthen the position of Serbia. For once the Serbs can claim to be victims and officially point out that the status of the province is still under the jurisdiction of Belgrade. Times are changing, and KFOR will not be around forever. Recall the words of General Nebosja Pavkovic, commander of the 3rd Army during the Serbian retreat from Kosovo: "We shall return to Kosovo if the treaty signed with NATO fails." One thing is certain, on the scale of time and the Balkans, Serbia has always been the dominant power in the region.

French paratroops of the 4ème Compagnie of the 3ème RPIMa (Régiment Parachutiste d'Infanterie de Marine – Regiment of Marine Infantry Paratrooper).

A member of the GCP, an elite "pathfinder", relaxes after a patrol. Note the equipment, including the K-bar knife, attached to the webbing, as well as the camouflage on the FAMAS, which is equipped with a 40mm grenade launcher.

These French paras were photographed at Gate 1, the post located at the border of Serbia.

This soldier presents the typical appearance of a French paratrooper of the 3ème RPIMa. The only difference in appearance between him and a metropolitan paratrooper is the beret badge featuring the Marine anchor on a winged sword. The RPIMa is the successor to the RPC (Régiment Parachutiste Coloniaux – Colonial Paratrooper Regiment), which changed its name after the war in Algeria.

A section (platoon) of the 4ème Compagnie of the 3ème RPIMa conducts a short briefing before going out on patrol in Leposavic, a small Serbian town north of Mitrovica.

The ethnic makeup of the town of Leposavic is 99% Serbian, so no problems have been reported in the area.

All of the soldiers in the section are dressed in full combat dress with flak jackets and heavy helmets.

Two NCOs of the 4th Company of the 3rd RPIMa patrol the streets of Leposavic. The nickname of the company is "Leopard," and it was this company, along with the 3rd Company from the same regiment, who launched the largest heliborne assault since the Algerian war when, in 1999, they captured the city of Vucitirn south of Mitrovica.

The "metropolitan" badge, which does not feature the Marine anchor, is shown to advantage on the red beret worn by the lieutenant in the background. The trident badge seen on the shoulder patch of the officer in the foreground is the badge of the MNB-NW.

French paras of the 1er RCP (Régiment de Chasseurs Parachutistes) light infantry regiment disembark from a Berliet truck. Due to the rapid deployment of the company to Kosovo in an urgent airlift, the 1er RCP did not have its own vehicles. It was compelled to use old Berliet trucks borrowed from the logistic units.

Paratroopers of the 1er Compagnie of the 1er RCP patrol in a village southeast of Mitrovica. One side of the street is Albanian and the other is Serbian, but no tension exists in this village. Problems arise only when people from other village get involved.

The newly arrived paratroops exchange impressions with the ground troops that were involved in the events.

This young para of the 1er RCP wears Arktiss web gear, which he bought with his own money and is very popular among elite European troops. The paras do not like to wear the heavy helmet because they believe that their red beret is a psychological weapon.

The trucks at the checkpoint are parked at an angle to the curb to break the speed of any car that would try to force its way through. Note the shotgun worn by the NCO, who is also armed with a FAMAS.

These paratroops, which belong to the 1er Compagnie of the 1er RCP, took up a position a few hundred meters from the checkpoint to protect it. Note the FR-F2 sniping rifle in the background. As in all of the units in the French Army (and even some in other Western armies), the units are overextended. For example, one GCP team of the 1st RCP was in Afghanistan, the 1er Compagnie and the other GCP team in Kosovo, the 2ème Compagnie in Gaboon, the 3ème Compagnie and Support Coy in Haiti, and the 4ème Compagnie in Ivory Coast. Thus, the 1er RCP was dispatched to four continents.

Paratroopers of the 1er RCP set up a checkpoint near Vucitirn.

The other unit that arrived in Kosovo as reinforcements is a company of the Belgian 1er Lanciers (1st Lancers), a Leopard tank regiment of the Belgian 16th Mechanized Brigade. They are seen here in position at the "Cambronne" bridge in Mitrovica. Note the "barbecue" hill in the background.

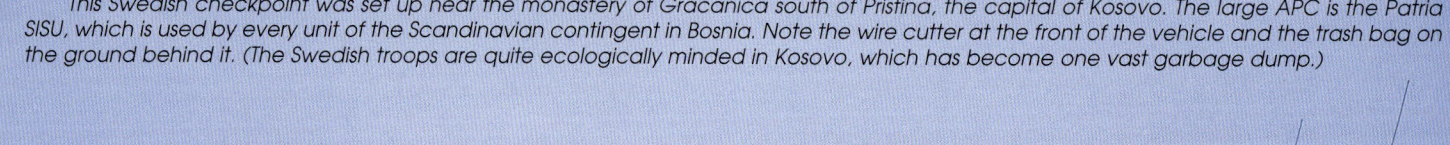

This Unimog light truck belongs to the Belgian 1st Lancers Regiment. Note the protection of the windscreen and the large national flag on the door of the cab.

This Swedish checkpoint was set up near the monastery of Gracanica south of Pristina, the capital of Kosovo. The large APC is the Patria SISU, which is used by every unit of the Scandinavian contingent in Bosnia. Note the wire cutter at the front of the vehicle and the trash bag on the ground behind it. (The Swedish troops are quite ecologically minded in Kosovo, which has become one vast garbage dump.)

Swedish soldiers stand guard at the checkpoint in Gracanica.

This 13th century monastery at Ducane, which contains the grave of Stefan Ducan, one of the first Serbian kings, was destroyed by the crowd of rioting Albanians.

German Dingo armored trucks sit in front of the UNMIK building at Prizren. The Albanian crowd also attacked this building.

The Dingo was especially made for service in the Balkans

The first batch of 56 Dingos (including 44 for Bosnian service) was ordered in 2000, a second batch of 57 (including five for the Special Forces) was ordered one year later, and a third batch of 34 was ordered in 2003.

A machine gunner in position atop a Dingo armored truck. The weapon is the classic MG3, a descendant of the famous MG42 of World War Two. The soldier wears the beret of a Panzergrenadier. It is difficult to say exactly which unit of the German contingent he is from because it contains a mixture of various units, but it was Panzergrenadierbrigade 41 that assumed command of the MND-SW during the March event. The main units are Panzergrenadierbataillon 411 and Panzerbataillon 403.

The Dingo is also in service in Afghanistan with the German troops of IFOR.

*A German checkpoint on the "Lion" road not far from the famous monastery at Ducane. The mountains in the background are the border between Kosovo, Albania and Macedonia (FYROM) and also serve as route for smuggling. The Dingo is probably from the third batch because it wears NATO's three-color camouflage.*

*A German Panzergrenadier is seen in Prizren. He is armed with a G36 assault rifle fitted with a 40mm grenade launcher.*

*Several historic buildings in Prizren were burned during the uprising. The German soldiers did not have clear orders to prevent the burning because the chain of command of KFOR was neglected in favor of the German government itself. The latter was afraid and obsessed with the "zero deaths" attitude.*

*An Italian soldier in Prizren. Due to the reduction in the number of troops, the former MNB-West under command of the Italians and the MNB-South West under command of the Germans were combined in November of 2002. The new MNB-South West numbers some 7500 men from 13 nations.*

*An Italian Land Rover Defender sits at the side of a road in the mountainous terrain of Kosovo.*

*For two years the British did not send any additional troops to Kosovo, but following the eruption of violence, they deployed a battalion of the Wiltshire Regiment. Here they are seen preparing to go out on patrol in Pristina.*

*A Ukrainian recce detachment under command of the U.S.-led MNB-East guards a mountain pass on the "Lion" road. They are equipped with BRDM-2s and this interesting version of the Humvee fitted with a Degtyarev 12.7mm heavy machine gun and an armored roof.*

# Aussies in Baghdad

Yves Debay

*The troops in the 2nd Cavalry Regiment operate three LAVs (ASLAV-25mm) and one Bison APC that is very similar to the Canadian version.*

Only one month after the fall of Baghdad, the embassies of Jordan, Turkey and Italy were the targets of a brand new resistance force. The admitted purpose of the rocket and mortar attacks was to dissuade other countries from developing diplomatic ties with the new temporary government, which was established by the coalition and which had no popular base [1]. On 19 August 2003, a booby-trapped truck exploded at UN headquarters, killing twenty-four people. To this violence add the murder of diplomats such as the Spanish military attaché, which forced Madrid to evacuate its diplomatic staff in November 2003. This "war of embassies"

would encourage certain countries to deploy a real contingent to protect their diplomatic representation. This was notably the case with Australia, which became part of the war against terrorism launched by U.S. President George W. Bush.

Special forces personnel from the Australian Defence Force had already been deployed to Afghanistan, and other military elements were present in the Middle East in preparation for possible action against Iraq. Among them were 150 or so personnel deployed with two P-3C Orion maritime patrol aircraft, 150 personnel with three RAAF C-130 Hercules transport aircraft, 70 personnel responsible for coordinating air operations, and 600 personnel embarked on two Royal Australian Navy frigates. The latter assured naval fire support during operations on the Fao Peninsula.

(1)   One of the main grievances of the average Iraqi has been that the responsibility given to the members of this temporary government was decided by the Americans. These leaders, who are mainly Shi'ites and Kurds, are not popular.

Australian snipers have taken up positions on the roof of the Carthage Hotel. From this position the Australians can view all of southeast Baghdad. The Australian snipers are armed with the classic Accuracy International PM sniper rifle. Fed by a 10-round box magazine, the bolt-action rifle fires 7.62 x 51mm NATO ammunition. The weapon weighs 6.5kg (14.3 lb) and is 112.4-119.4 cm (44-47 inches) long. Its barrel alone is 65.5 cm (26 inches) long. The rifle, which has a two-stage trigger that is adjustable to 1-2kg, is fitted with a Schmidt & Bender PM6x42 sight.

A combat and observation post of the 2nd Battalion of the Royal Australian Regiment is organized on one of the top floors of the Carthage Hotel. The weapon is the popular MINIMI machine gun.

Another combat and observation post atop the Carthage Hotel. This site is armed with an FN MAG machine gun.

Australia paid dearly for her support of the coalition; it was mainly Australian nationals who were targeted in a subsequent bombing attack in Bali that claimed the lives of 250 people. Officially, Australia is a part of the coalition, but her soldiers are not integrated into the coalition force. However, this does not protect the nation (or any nation maintaining links to the new government) from threats. So Canberra takes very seriously the task of protecting the embassy in Baghdad, sending a special detachment of troops to do so. As of the spring of 2004, the Australian presence in Iraq and the region is limited to 850 personnel, including a security company in charge of protecting the embassy, a command platoon, and the detachment of air controllers at the Baghdad Airport, which includes 60 people. The latter have often been witness to numerous attacks on the airport.

In the city we find Chief Warrant Officer Horn, who commands the security company. "Welcome to Townsville Base," he says. The name was not chosen with much imagination but its location is remarkable. It is situated in the "Carthage Hotel" in construction that adjoins the embassy in the Al Qadisyah residential area. It is here where the officer set up his command post, where he receives his orders directly from the frigate *HMAS Melbourne* [2], which patrols in the Arabian Gulf. Its mission is simple: Assure the protection of the Australian nationals and their interests in Iraq.

From the summit of the Carthage Hotel, which consists simply of a simple concrete frame of about twenty floors, the "Aussies" have a

The machine gunner is absent from this combat and observation post, but the observer keeps a sharp lookout with his Steyr AUG fitted with a 40mm grenade launcher at the ready.

(2)    The frigates *HMAS Newcastle* and *HMAS Melbourne* took part in operations. These vessels are regularly called to service.

*Some of the 15 soldiers belonging to the 2nd Cavalry Regiment gather outside the Carthage Hotel.*

magnificent panoramic view of the capital that extends for miles. Snipers who have taken up position with their accurate rifles on one of the upper floors are ready to counter any threat to the embassy. This spot is also a perfect observation platform, and during the night the Australian soldiers often witness attacks against the "Green Zone" [3]. Although it goes beyond the scope of their mission, it is likely that from this impregnable vantage point the Australians report their observations to the HQ of the coalition.

(3)    Green Zone: Vast area where the Americans have settled in the complex of Saddam Hussein's palaces and the Al Rashad Hotel along the Tigris River. The Green Zone also includes the Sheraton and Palestine Hotels on the other side of the river, which are regularly the targets of mortar and rocket attacks.

*Far from simply sitting idle, the Australian troops from the 2nd Cavalry Regiment are actually biding their time prior to serving as an armed escort.*

*The Carthage Hotel is located in a residential suburb. Note the LAV armored vehicle on the road outside the hotel.*

*The Australian soldiers in Iraq are dressed in desert camouflage uniforms just like those worn in Afghanistan by the Canberra special forces. The participation of Australia on the side of the Americans in the war against terrorism is important.*

*This band of troops from the 2nd Battalion of the Royal Australian Regiment is part of a platoon of Australian troops that is composed of thirty soldiers.*

*This Australian soldier is holding a MINIMI light machine gun, which is now the standard light machine gun of many Western countries. The famous Belgian weapon has a caliber of 5.56mm x 45 (FN SS 109 NATO or M193) and can be fed its ammunition from 200-round belts or from 30-round M-16A1 magazines.*

Written on the walls, one serviceman points out, are Arabic characters that translate as encouragement for Iraqis to die as martyrs. On the bottom of a flyer sent out from various departments is the warning "Remember these characters. They were found on the car that committed a suicide attack that almost destroyed the Italian embassy."

The security company consists of an infantry platoon supplied by the 2nd Battalion of the Royal Australian Regiment, a command platoon and a troop of the 2nd Cavalry Regiment. The mission of this troop is to protect the ambassador and his guests, and the rare Australian nationals, as they move in and out of the city, if the situation should turn bad (which is always possible). The 15 members of the troop are equipped with four LAV light, wheeled, armored personnel carriers.

In charge of the main mission to guard the embassy are 30 members of the 2nd Battalion of the Royal Australian Regiment. The Australian soldiers have an impressive armament at their disposal: Steyr AUG assault rifles (some of which are fitted with 40mm grenade launchers), FN, MINIMI, FN MAG, and sniper rifles. Many of these weapons are fitted with the F88 Night Aiming Device (NAD) for the Steyr AUG and the F89 for the machine guns.

This brief discussion of the Australian contingent would not be complete without the mention of a small detachment of three pioneers specialized in explosives and six imposing MPs in charge of close protection of the ambassador. Ready to repel any terrorist attack, the modest Australian contingent is well aware that they are privileged to witness the turnover that is presently shaking up the Middle East.

*A combat group from the 2nd Battalion of the Royal Australian Regiment prepares to conduct a patrol in the vicinity of the Australian embassy. Rising skyward in the background is the Carthage Hotel.*

*Because of its design, the barrel of the F88 (Steyr AUG) can be changed from a short barrel to a longer one (70.9cm (28 inches)). The weapon is the first assault rifle to make extensive use of plastic in its manufacture.*

*The standard weapon used in the Australian Army is the F88, which is the Steyr AUG manufactured under license in Australia. The standard circular graticule covers a height of 1.8 meters (6 feet) at 300 meters (328 yards). As the photo illustrates, the "bull pup" design makes the F88 an extremely short weapon, with a barrel of only 50.8cm (20 inches). The weapon pictured is also fitted with a 40mm grenade launcher.*

A MINIMI light machine gun is mounted on top of a light armored vehicle. Weighing 6.85kg (15 lb) and measuring 104cm (41inches) in length, the weapon has a muzzle velocity of 965 m/s and a rate of fire (cyclic) of 700-1000 rounds per minute.

Australian MPs are armed with the F88 assault rifle, as well as a 9mm pistol holstered at their side.

This MP is one member of a six-man team tasked with the close protection of the Australian ambassador. The Australian MPs are issued special equipment. Note his MP brassard, chest webbing and radio headset.

In view of the danger foreign embassy personnel face in Iraq, the MPs who offer protection to the Australian ambassador must be the highest caliber of soldier. These men certainly display a professional demeanor.

*The Light Armored Vehicles and the Bison APC are used for escort service in the city of Baghdad.*

*Note the Australian three-tone "bush" camouflage on the Australian armored vehicles. The weapon fitted to the top of the turret is the Belgian FN MAG.*

# Street Fights in Grozny

James R. Hill

## The Evolution of Russian Urban Combat in Chechnya

Performing an act of compassion that would be repeated many times, Russian soldiers evacuate a wounded comrade from combat amid the rubble and ruins of Grozny. The Russians learned quickly that victory in Chechnya would come at a high cost, if it came at all. (Novosti)

The Soviet Union's war in Afghanistan in the 1980s was an earlier attempt to stabilize a friendly Marxist government in a strategic part of the world. This scene showing Red Army soldiers being treated to watermelon by a local took place in Hushka, Turkmenistan in Afghanistan in October of 1986. (Novosti)

September 3, 2003, in the northern Caucasus region of Russia, two bombs exploded under a train that was transporting students to school. Six of them were killed and 50 were wounded. A similar blast in southern Russia on December 5, 2003 on a commuter train killed 44 people and wounded at least 150. Four days later, another blast rocked Moscow when a suicide bomber detonated explosives near the Kremlin and killed a number of passers-by. On August 24, 2004, two Russian passenger planes crashed within minutes of each other, killing 90 passengers and crew.

More recently, at the beginning of September of 2004, gunmen seized a school in Beslan, in southern Russia. They took more than 1000 hostages, many of them children, holding them prisoner in the gymnasium where they strung explosives above their heads. After a 3-day standoff, the explosives were detonated and the gunmen shot as many hostages as they could before being subdued. More than 320 of the hostages perished; 727 of them were wounded.

These are but a few of the violent acts of terrorism perpetrated over the last few years that are rooted in the ongoing conflict in the Russian province of Chechnya.

Russia has been involved in an on again/off again war with rebels in Chechnya since 1994. This war produced three major attempts to capture the capital of Chechnya, the city of Grozny, in an effort to quell what the government in Moscow called a rebellion, and what the Chechen separatists regard as a struggle for independence. The fighting for Grozny served as a test of the abilities of the Russian Armed Forces to successfully wage urban combat. This article will study the outcome of that test.

*Soviet soldiers relax while they and the rows of tanks behind them wait their turn to be sent home from Afghanistan. The Soviets pulled out of Afghanistan in two steps, one in 1988 and one in 1989, after nearly a decade of fighting and without having achieved their goal of putting down the rebellion against the communist regime in that nation. (Novosti)*

### Background

When the Union of Soviet Socialist Republics (USSR) collapsed in 1991, the world witnessed an event that few people thought they would see in their lifetime. The USSR had consisted of 14 Union Republics and 20 Autonomous Republics. Soon all but one of the Union Republics gained independence and formed a new nation, the Russian Federation. Though independent states, they were still influenced by the Russian government in Moscow. Chechnya, which was an Autonomous Republic, balked at becoming a part of the new Russian Federation.

Dzhokhar Dudayev, a former general in the Soviet Air Force, was elected president of Chechnya. Once in power he took the bold step of declaring Chechnya an independent nation. Though Russia did not initially oppose Chechnya's bid for independence, Russian President Boris Yeltsin came to view Chechnya's attitude as a threat to the stability of the rest of Russia. He refused to recognize Chechen independence and ordered troops into Chechnya to end what he viewed as a rebellion.

The relationship between Chechnya and the Russian government has been rife with bad feelings. In the 1830s, when Czar Nicholas I invaded the Caucasus, he met stiff resistance. In 1944, Stalin deported thousands of Chechens to Siberia in the belief that they were collaborating with the Nazis. When Yeltsin ordered a military incursion into the region, the Chechens were primed for a fight . . . and they got one.

While combat occurred in locations other than in Grozny, the evolution of Russian urban combat techniques can best be evaluated by looking at the three main operations aimed at conquering that city. These took place in 1994, 1996 and 2000.

### Grozny – 1994/1995

On December 11, 1994, Russian troops invaded Chechnya and moved on the capital city of Grozny. During World War Two, the Soviet Army successfully conducted urban warfare while fighting in and around Stalingrad and during the conquest of Berlin. However, as the advance against Grozny progressed, it became obvious that the Russian military

*Soldiers who may be members of the Democratic Army of Afghanistan cover the muzzle of a tank's gun at the end of Soviet involvement in Afghanistan. The fall of communism in the USSR silenced many a gun. . . at least for a time. (Novosti)*

35

In December 1994, Russian tanks once again took up an aggressive role when the Russian army was sent into Chechnya. These are some of the 2200 tanks that participated in some way in the first battle for Grozny in 1994/1995. (Novosti)

commanders would not be drawing upon this wealth of historical experience to help them in the fight in Chechnya.

While the Chechens anticipated a fight when the Russian tanks, armored vehicles, and troops arrived on the outskirts of the city, the Russian troops certainly did not. The Russian force, which numbered about 5,000, advanced into Grozny boldly and without caution, contemptible of the ability of the Chechen rebels to pose any real threat and apparently oblivious to the anger that had been seething within the breasts of the Chechen people. In fact, Yeltsin had been advised that it would take as little as 24 hours to quell the rebellion in Chechnya! This Russian force was a combination of Russian army, air force and Ministry of the Interior (MVD, a kind of National Guard) troops that were thrown together quickly without proper training. Waiting for them was more or less an equal force of determined, well-prepared and well-armed Chechens. Some of them were former soldiers in the Red Army, which

Chechen rebels on the move. Far from being the rabble that much of the Russian leadership thought would be subdued in days, the Chechens were a well-trained, motivated foe who fought stubbornly and skillfully. The man wearing the helmet carries a rocket-propelled grenade (RPG) launcher, a weapon that was used with deadly success against Russian armored vehicles during the first battle for Grozny. (Novosti)

Russian soldiers dressed in heavy winter uniforms and ushanka wool caps gather around a small fire and prepare for battle. Many of the Russian troops pulled together for the invasion of Chechnya were poorly trained and new to combat. (Novosti)

The bleak winter landscape in Chechnya was made even less attractive when war began to ravage dwellings and buildings. This photograph serves as a reminder that the fighting was not limited to cities like Grozny but took place in more rural areas as well. (Novosti)

Dressed in camouflage, Russian combatants pose for a photograph amid bed frames, bedding and pillows that were confiscated for use by the army. The fellow seated in the middle wearing a black knit cap has a blue and white striped shirt under his jacket, which indicates that he belongs to an airborne or naval infantry unit. (Novosti)

gave them some insight into the thinking of their opponent and a familiarity with enemy equipment. These rebels had spent months familiarizing themselves with the layout of the city above and below ground. By contrast, the Russian troops, many of whom were inexperienced conscripts, had received no urban combat training, and the commanders had conducted only limited reconnaissance regarding the city and its inhabitants.

Preliminary air strikes were launched to knock out key targets, but these bombings did not serve their purpose. In fact, the civilian deaths that resulted only aggravated the anti-Russian sentiment. With no support from

artillery or aircraft, a number of Russian tanks led the way into Grozny, with soldiers following. The Chechen fighters took advantage of this faulty tactic. Armed with rocket-propelled grenade (RPG) launchers, they knocked out the tanks in the front and rear of the columns. (The Chechens knew just where to hit the tanks – at the base or on top of the turret – to cripple them). Thus bottled up, the Russian troops who tried to escape from the trapped armored vehicles were killed or taken prisoner. In the first

What could be the skeletal remnants of a building in Stalingrad during World War Two are probably the ruins of a portion of Grozny. The bombardment by artillery and air that was heaped upon that city was devastating. Despite the destruction, the Chechens found many hiding places from which to harass the Russian forces. (Novosti)

*Visibly fatigued, Russian troops take the rare opportunity to rest. Mental exhaustion also took a heavy toll on the troops, particularly in the 1994/1995 battle for Grozny. The physical and mental health of the Russian soldiers worsened once they were introduced to the demands of urban combat. One survey showed that nearly of the troops tested suffered from some kind of psychological problem. (Novosti)*

*A weary soldier cooks up a meager meal. By February 1995, the Russian troops had become woefully familiar with the sufferings of warfare. The Russian logistics system was unable to provide the troops with drinking and dishwashing water. As a result, illness was widespread, with viral hepatitis and cholera topping the least of maladies that beset the troops. (Novosti)*

*This youthful Russian soldier is typical of the troops that were sent into Chechnya and who fought in Grozny in 1994. Many were conscripts who knew little of war and less about the politics of the region. Unsure of the reason they were there, some found it difficult to view the Chechen people as enemies. (Novosti)*

three days of fighting, the Russians lost 400 tanks.

In another part of Grozny, Russian tanks and infantry belonging to an advance unit of the Maikop Brigade advanced as far as the railroad station downtown and stopped. Some troops wandered around. Others relaxed. No one expected trouble. But suddenly Chechen fighters descended on them. Occupying the basement level and upper floors of surrounding buildings, the Chechen rebels remained out of reach of the Russian tanks, which could not lower or raise their gun barrels enough to hit those floors. After several hours of fighting, the Russians found themselves running low on ammunition. With no reinforcements available, they fought their way out of the train station and harm's way at great loss.

The Chechen force proved to be a far more formidable foe than expected, operating in small hunter-killer teams consisting of an RPG gunner, machine gunner and sniper. They made the most of their familiarity with their home terrain and the advantage of being the defender. They also put cell phones, the Internet, radios, and video cameras to good use in order to remain in communication with each other. They also stayed in such close physical proximity to the Russian troops (using a tactic called "hugging") that the full force of the Russian artillery and air power could

not be employed without killing their own men. The separatists further trumped the Russians by staying mobile and driving all over the city to create the illusion of being a much larger force. They had some access in and out of Grozny since the Russians had failed to completely surround the city. Further, Chechen soldiers were skilled at setting booby-traps and mines, employing such varied means and items that the Russians were consistently caught off guard. Even the bodies of both Russian and Chechen soldiers were often booby-trapped.

This initial Chechen success did not last long because the Russians eventually started to employ basic urban combat tactics. Tossing grenades through both the door and windows, the Russians would capture one building at a time, make sure it was secure, and then move on to the next building. Troops that were more experienced would lead the assault and less experienced troops would provide support. Smaller, more portable cannon were put into action instead of the bulky tanks that had proved such easy prey.

Early in the conflict the Russians communicated via unsecured radio and language, and the Chechens had no trouble intercepting their messages. Once the Soviet force began sending coded messages their communication was far more secure. Other equipment was adopted to thwart the Chechen rebels. At night the Russians used illumination rounds fired by artillery to identify enemy troops and blind them. In contrast, the Russians used night vision goggles to retain their own vision in the dark of night.

The Russian army also developed the use of assault groups that operated on a smaller, more intimate scale and which directed air fire. Weather permitting, the air force could lend its support by dropping laser-

*Destruction and desolation are the ultimate by-products of urban warfare. Grozny was no exception. In order for the Russians to finally capture wrest control of the city from the Chechens, they first had to demolish it. (Novosti)*

guided bombs on specific targets. This was an obvious improvement over cluster bombs, whose deadly use in the first days of the conflict had served only to anger formerly loyal civilians.

Cooperation among the various branches of the Russian armed forces (paratroops, elite troops and air force) had been lacking the first several days of combat. But during the first week of January 1995, Russian aircraft annihilated Chechen troops and tanks that were attempting to maneuver from the city. Artillery units working in conjunction with *spetsnaz* and other Soviet elite forces inflicted heavy blows against the rebel forces. Still the Chechens resisted. They even used misinformation as a weapon, sending fake informants to feed false leads to the Russians, and dressing in civilian dress or Russian army uniforms to mingle among the Soviet troops. Often the only way to distinguish rebels from civilians was to search their pockets for military documents, check their shoulder blades for bruises caused by the recoil of weapons, examine their forearms for

*Russian soldiers fire on Chechen positions in a suburb of Grozny in this photograph that was taken in January of 1995. On January 15, the Russians finally succeeded in surrounding the Chechen capital and closing off the city. (Novosti)*

*Sadly, civilians rarely escape the brutalities of war. Soldiers often mistreat or kill civilians, and those who survive the fighting are displaced from their homes and are sometimes separated from loved ones. It is estimated that by 2000, the fighting in Chechnya had created 250,000 refugees, many of whom were former residents of Grozny. (Novosti)*

*A soldier belonging to the Russian Interior Ministry (MVD) force watches as an oil storage tank belches black smoke skyward as it burns somewhere in Chechnya in 1995. (Novosti)*

*MVD troops prepare to destroy an ammunition dump that was captured from the Chechen separatist forces. Besides their automatic weapons, the Chechens had at their disposal RPG-7 anti-tank grenade launchers, 120mm cannons, Grad rocket launchers, SA-7 and SA-14 surface-to-air missile launchers, and grenades. (Novosti)*

Nevertheless, Moscow considered the battle for Grozny to be a Russian victory since the city was taken and resistance crushed (at least for the time being), but losses were staggering. The Russians lost 2,805 killed, 10,319 wounded and 393 missing in action, and 133 captured.

Real victory in the context of urban combat often depends on the performance of the occupying force after the fighting has ended. Although 10,000 Russian troops occupied Grozny after it was captured, they failed to adequately secure the city or keep an effective watch over the points of entry. They did not help to restore utilities and other public necessities such as transportation, sanitation, water, food, etc. and some of the behavior of the troops toward the civilians alienated rather than reconciled them. All of these shortcomings combined to create a prelude to further disaster.

### Grozny – 1996

Between 1994 and 1996, a number of smaller conflicts erupted between the Chechens and the Russians. In 1995, Chechen leader Dudayev was himself killed by a Russian rocket. In March 1996, the Chechens made a formal move to retake Grozny. On March 6, the Chechen commander, Chamil Busayev, and 500 of his men arrived by train in Grozny then disbursed to look for the Russian MVD troop positions. Five days of heavy fighting ensued, and two hundred Russian troops were lost before the efforts of the would-be re-conquerors were thwarted.

On August 6, two smaller groups of 60 Chechens captured the railway station in Grozny and other key positions throughout the city. Some four thousand combatants reinforced them. Soon they took possession of the three main routes leading into downtown Grozny. The MVD troops were unable to defend against this well-orchestrated operation. The next day, Russian troops stationed outside the city slowly responded to the emergency. Apparently learning little from the first struggle for Grozny, they sent vehicles, including a tank, in the open down a road toward the city; of course they were destroyed.

On August 11, more tanks entered downtown Grozny. Supported by artillery, they slowly began the effort to recapture the city. Two weeks of bloody combat took place before negotiations brought the fighting to a close on August 22. The terms of the negotiations called for the departure of the Russians from Grozny. This short, but bloody second battle for Grozny resulted in the Russians losing 500 dead and 1400 wounded or missing . . . and the Chechens gaining control of their capital city once again.

powder burns, or smell them to try to detect the odor of gunpowder and gun oil.

Between January 10 and 12, the Russians made use of a cease-fire that they themselves declared (but did not honor) to reinforce and resupply the Soviet troops. On January 12, following a three-hour barrage of rockets that rained down on Grozny, the Russians launched an offensive against the downtown area, which represented the heart of the separatist movement. Particular landmarks that saw the worst fighting were the presidential palace and the railroad station. On January 15, the Russians finally succeeded in surrounding Grozny and isolating the city. On January 18, the Russian flag was raised above the presidential palace, where Chechen president Dudayev had lived, and it was soon blown up; this was more of a psychological than a tactical blow against the Chechens.

On January 26, the commander of the interior forces of the MVD was given overall command of the Russian forces fighting for Grozny. Combat continued in the outskirts of town for several more weeks. By the end of Janaury, 1995, most of the resistance was centered near Minutka Square, an important crossroads southeast of the presidential palace. Using Shmel rocket launchers that fire thermobaric rounds, the Russians eliminated one pocket of resistance after another. By February 5, Minutka Square and the southern roads leading into Grozny were under Russian control. The Chechens continued to launch assaults through late February 1995, but once the Russians began to encircle the rebels the Chechen commander concluded it was time to abandon Grozny. It should be noted that he did not consider this withdrawal to be any kind of route or total defeat.

A Russian armored unit advances along a street in Grozny in March 1996 after the Chechens launched an offensive to retake the city. It took five days of combat before the Russians could foil this attempt to reclaim the capital. (Novosti)

The Russians withdrew from Grozny and, ultimately, from Chechnya, but they did not go far. A sizable Soviet military force remained in the north Caucasus near Chechnya to practice anti-guerilla tactics in the mountains. One particular type of training was glaringly absent – tactics for urban combat. Basing their decision on the two prior bloody failures in Grozny, the Russian military commanders concluded that they would avoid urban combat in the future and, therefore, not train their troops for that eventuality.

## Grozny – 2000

In the late summer/early fall of 1999, the Russians were drawn back into Chechnya in response to the actions of Chechen insurgents who entered the Russian territory of Dagestan to help Islamic fundamentalists create a separate nation. Bombings of several buildings in Russia were blamed on the Chechens, and public opinion turned decidedly negative against Chechnya. The new prime minister, Vladimir Putin, decided to send a force of more than 100,000 men (80,000 ground troops from the

Not all destruction was limited to the urban areas in Chechnya. In June 1996, this cordon of Russian soldiers (background) was photographed in the countryside passing by the remains of the demolished armored vehicle that stands as a mute warning of the danger that awaits them. (Novosti)

Russian troops prepare to go out on a combat mission in June 1996. Prior to the main incursion conducted by the Chechens in August 1996, a number of smaller engagements took place between the Russians and the Chechen fighters. (Novosti)

In August 1996, the Chechens infiltrated Grozny to attack key positions held by the Interior Ministry troops. Unable to repulse the attack, the Russian army was forced to turn possession of the city back over to the Chechens. Here Chechen fighters take advantage of a break in the fighting to reload ammunition belts near a house in central Grozny from which they conducted their defensive operations. (Novosti)

Ministry of Defense and 30,000 from the MVD) into Chechnya to eliminate the terrorist threat. The Chechen capital city of Grozny was once again a prime target.

The Russian force that prepared to assault Grozny in this instance was varied indeed. Participating along with the MVD and regular army troops were elite *spetsnaz* elements, units of naval infantry commandos, and combined forces of infantry, armor, artillery, NBC units, marksmen, engineers, and helicopter units. Of special note is that this time the Russians had the assistance of Chechen militiamen under the command of the one-time mayor of Grozny, Bislan Gantemirov, who wanted to restore order in the city. These Chechen allies were able to obtain accurate and useful intelligence from local civilians; it is highly unlikely that the Russian troops could have done so.

By December 1999, Grozny was totally surrounded. Though it would not be completely effective, the blockade around the city was much tighter this time around than in 1995. Also, the Russians thoroughly studied city maps and other papers to acquaint themselves with its streets, sewage lines and public utility sites. Having taken to heart the lessons learned from the first two battles for the city, the Russian military commanders decided not to barge in as they had done previously. For two months Russian artillery and aircraft bombed and shelled selected targets in Chechnya such as relay towers and communication facilities to isolate the Chechen fighters in Grozny as much as possible from support outside the city.

In mid-December, the Russians made a tentative advance into Grozny. A reconnaissance force that had mustered on the outskirts of town in mid-November sent a number of small recon units and combat engineers to deploy within the city to gather information. Sniper teams supported by the army and MVD also took up positions in the city to find targets and gather further useful information on the location and movement of Chechen troops. They also served as spotters for artillery that ringed the city.

This time when the Russians conducted their assault on various locations within the city, the ground troops advanced on foot in support of armored personnel carriers that were often armed with grenade launchers. When Chechen snipers were spotted, the automatic fire from the armored vehicle eliminated the threat. Generally, though, armored vehicles were kept out of the city during this fight for Grozny. Assault groups composed of about 50 men, which were broken up into smaller units of three or so armed with an RPG and an assault weapon, searched out the main points of resistance and called in artillery or air strikes. This fire direction from lower echelon troops was a new and effective step forward in urban combat for the Russians.

Most of the population of Chechnya is Muslim, so the guns of the Chechen fighters are silent during daily prayers. It was Chechen fighters going to the support of Islamic fundamentalist separatists in Dagestan in 2000 that provided the Russians the incentive to once again move into Chechnya. Note the interesting combination of camouflage worn by this Chechen. (I. Mikhalev)

Heavy fighting took place late in December 1999 and lasted throughout January 2000. Regular MVD troops, accompanied by special MVD units (Special Purpose Police Detachment [OMON] and Special Rapid Reaction Detachment [SOBR]), were the first to move toward the downtown area, but regular ground forces later added their support. Before long the Russians had captured the main bridge over the Sunja River. True to form, the Chechens fought tenaciously. They employed many of the same tactics (small-unit operations, "hugging", snipers, using sewer system for rapid mobility) that had served them so well during the other two conflicts in Grozny. Often at night they would re-occupy the buildings or positions from which they had been driven during the day.

During January 2000, the fighting centered in Minutka Square, a key position where roads and communication lines intersected. The Russians launched an operation to capture the multi-floor buildings that overlooked the square and gave safe haven to snipers. Well-coordinated attacks by assault groups using mortars and RPGs helped them to secure a few of the buildings, including one with nine stories, but it was lost to a Chechen counterattack.

The size of the Russian force during this contest for Grozny proved too large for the Chechens to overcome. On 2 February 2000, after three weeks of bitter resistance, the Chechen fighters once again abandoned the city of Grozny and literally headed for the hills. The MVD's Special Purpose Police were tasked with sweeping the neighborhoods of Grozny to root out any diehard Chechen fighters. Some sporadic fighting took place, but my March 2000 the battle for Grozny was over.

Russian forces were back in Grozny by the spring of 2000. During the third battle for the city, the Russians tried not move in their armored vehicles until smaller reconnaissance units had located and eliminated pockets of rebel resistance. When armored vehicles did operate in the city, they were protected by ground troops. (V. Vyatkin)

### Improved Tactics

The Russians took a number of steps other than those already mentioned to succeed in their capture of Grozny in 2000. From the very beginning, the government in Moscow controlled the media reports of the latest Chechen conflict to ensure that public opinion remained favorable. Communications among the Russian military units were kept more secure through the use of the Akveduk radio, which allowed every soldier to send encrypted messages. They also communicated misleading information to the Chechens. As the Russians were taking control of Grozny, some Chechen rebels were led out of the city and into a minefield and a massacre as a result of manipulation by false radio messages that suggested that a certain escape route was available to them.

Unlike the first battle for Grozny in 1994, the Russian military leaders permitted no cease-fires in the third battle, giving the Chechens no time to reorganize or resupply. They also saw to it that the Russian troops enjoyed more rest and relaxation to help them readjust emotionally and psychologically from the strain of urban combat. This desire to preserve the welfare of the soldiers led to new artillery tactics being employed. The artillery adopted a zonal-target method of firing that called for artillery and mortar batteries to support motorized rifle companies. Measures were also taken in 2000 to protect the troops from mines and booby traps. In February, after the Chechens departed Grozny, bomb disposal teams led the way into the city to hunt for mines that the Chechens had planted in buildings and on roads.

The Russians also conducted psychological operations against the civilians (distributing leaflets to encourage them to evacuate the city) and the Chechen fighters (broadcasting appeals for surrender through loudspeakers). The Russians also gained a psychological edge by employing SCUD missiles and fuel-air explosives (the 93mm "Bumblebee" flamethrower and the TOS-1, a flamethrower mounted on a T-72 chassis). These showed the Chechens, who could not combat these terrifying measures, that they could no longer be safe holed up in basements and subterranean hideaways.

The military conquest of Grozny in 2000 was not achieved without cost; one motorized regiment lost 25% of its strength. Nor was it by any means conducted flawlessly; there was still insufficient coordination during the MVD-regular armed forces joint operations, friend or foe identification was still inadequate, and the Chechens still managed to draw the Russians into unwanted close combat. But the victory in the third battle for Grozny demonstrated that Russian urban combat tactics had evolved remarkably and were effectively mature compared to those employed during the two catastrophic contests of 1994 and 1996.

In April of 2000 it seemed that a peaceful life was once again being restored to Grozny. Events since that time have proved that peace in Chechnya remains an unfulfilled dream. (V. Vyatkin)

43

# The Belgian
## Para-Commando Brigade

**Clemens Niesner**

*After the withdrawal of the 3rd Lanciers-Parachutists reconnaissance battalion, the Bombardier Iltis 4x4s were distributed among the three infantry battalions until they had built up their own recce platoons. This photograph shows a formidably camouflaged Iltis of the 2nd Commando Battalion from Flawinne.*

The armed forces of NATO partner Belgium actually consist of two mechanized brigades: 1st Mechanized Brigade at Leopoldsburg and 7th Mechanized Brigade at Marche-en-Famenne. The 17th Mechanized Brigade at Spich/Köln, the last Belgian garrison in Germany, was scheduled to be withdrawn at the end of 2003 following a large reorganization of the Belgian Armed Forces (Landcomponent 2015). Next to those mechanized brigades, the Para-Commando Brigade will be the third one providing airmobile capability.

### History and Development of the Para-Commando Brigade (Para Cdo Bde)

The Para-Commando Brigade was formed after World War Two by the amalgamation of two forces, the parachutists and the commandos. The first Belgian "paratrooper" company consisting of volunteers was established at the Royal School of Parachutists at Fritzhill, United Kingdom, on 8 May 1942. After two years of hard training, the "Belgian Squadron," which was commanded by Cpt. Blondeel, was put under the command of the famous SAS (Special Air Service) brigade.

Belgian paras began their first real combat action in 1944 in France, Belgium and the Dutch Friesland, and were involved in the Ardennes battles, most notably von Runstedt's Ardennes offensive. Following reorganization, the unit was named Belgium SAS Regiment. It was composed of three reconnaissance squads equipped with armored jeeps. One company supported 6th (UK) Para Division during recce and protection missions. At the same time, the first Belgian volunteer commando company, the 4th Troop commanded by 10th Commando, was formed at Acknacarry in Scotland. As the years passed, both arms slowly combined to finally become a para-commando regiment in 1952.

In an effort to maintain their identities and pay tribute to their roots, the designation "Parachutists (Para)" or "Commando (Cdo)" is included in each of the battalions' names.

An example is the 3 *Bataljon Parachutisten* (3rd Paratroopers Battalion), which was formed in 1955 by joining a detachment of 1 *Bataljon Parachutisten* (1st Paratroopers Battalion) and 2 *Bataljon*

*Each company in the infantry battalion consists of two fusilier (infantry) troops and an anti-tank troop equipped with Milan. Every troop has three groups of 10 soldiers each, equipped with one Minimi, one FNMAG 7.62mm, one Accuracy sniper rifle, and seven FNC 5.56mm assault rifles. Their vehicle is the Unimog 2-ton gl 1350L.*

For transport, the 475A1PRB 81mm mortars are disassembled and carried on a Unimog 2-ton 1350 gl in three parts that have a total weight of around 60kg (132 lb). Only 15 minutes pass from the time the mortars are mounted to the firing of the first shell!

Artillery support for each battalion is provided by six NR475A1 PRB 81mm mortars and about 570kg (1257 lb) of various ammunition. Enemy objectives can be engaged up to a distance of 3000 meters (3279 yards).

*Commandos* (2nd Commando Battalion), finally becoming 3 *Bataljon Parachutisten* when established in the Belgian Congo. The 3rd Paratroopers Battalion maintained the traditions of the Volunteer Korps in Korea, receiving special citations during the fighting in Korea that took place from 1951 to 1953. The Battalion proved its reliability during the struggle for independence in the Belgian Congo in 1960 and participated in airborne operations in Kikwit and Indu. The Battalion left its base in Burundi in 1962 and was deployed to Lombardsijde in Belgium.

During the Cold War, the Cdo Para Regiment was placed under the command of the Belgian Armed Land Forces, acting as a tactical defense reserve as well. The Regiment was further tasked with special assignments within NATO or to reinforce the former 1st (BE) Korps, the so-called " Earmarked Force," in Germany. Since the establishment of AMF(L)

Every infantry battalion has a reconnaissance unit consisting of one troop of "pathfinders" equipped with seven Bombardier Iltis vehicles. Besides the troop leader's vehicle, three more Iltis are used as recce vehicles. Three vehicles equipped with Milan ATGW provide the anti-tank element. A standard crew consists of a gunner armed with an Accuracy G-22 7.62mm sniper rifle, one soldier with an FNMAG 7.62mm gun mounted at the vehicle's right side and the driver with the FNC assault gun.

*The Pandur doesn't mind tough terrain. Here two vehicles of 16th Company, 2nd Commando Battalion easily negotiate a muddy tank track at Sennelager Training Center (STC) at Paderborn. The Pandur is designed to negotiate water obstacles up to a depth of 1.5m (1.6 yards). Thanks to its 275-liter (73-gallon) fuel tank, the vehicle has a range of about 700km (435 miles).*

(Allied Command Europe Mobile Force Land) in 1960, the Regiment has provided one battalion to the National Support Element, depending on its availability.

Over the years the Regiment successively received several units until it reached brigade strength in 1991. That same year, units of this new Para Cdo Bde participated in the FTX "Certain Shield 1991" of MNAD (Multinational Airmobile Division), which later became the MND(C) (Multinational Division Central Airmobile). Since then, the Para Cdo Bde has represented a major portion of MND(C) while also being part of the Belgian Intervention Force.

Soldiers of the Belgian Para Cdo Bde receive formidable training, a fact that they consistently prove when they participate in international military competitions. During Exercise "Aggressive Iron 2002," the last MND(C) exercise held before the withdrawal on 29 October from Mönchengladbach, the 2nd Commando Battalion won first place in the infantry competition just ahead of the 1.Jagers te Paard!

### The Brigade's Structure
Following the LANDCOMPONENT 2015 armed forces reorganization, even the Para-Cdo Bde will have to make a change and take on a new name, "Luchtmobiele Brigade."
The following units will be involved:
- Reconnaissance and Anti-Tank Battalion (3 L Para Cdo), Flawinne
- Air Defense Battery (35 Bij AA Para-Cdo), Spich
- Engineer Company (14 Cie Gn Para-Cdo), Herverlee
- Medical Company (16 Cie Med Para-Cdo), Herverlee
- Support Company (210 Cie Log Para-Cdo), Herverlee
Those units will be withdrawn or be given new tasks.

Even the Commando Training Center and the Parachutist School will be put under the Brigade's command. Between 2002 to 2005, these training devices will be reorganized for greater efficiency and flexibility.

The new structure of Luchtmobiele Brigade under LANDCOMPONENT 2015 will be:
- Headquarters with HQ Company, Herverlee
- Recce Troop (LRRP), Flawinne
- Special Forces Group (SF Gp), Flawinne
- *1ste Bataljon Parachutisten* with 13th, 17th and 22nd Company, Diest
- *2e Bataljon Commando* with 12th, 14th and 16th Company, Flawinne
- *3de Bataljon Parachutisten* with 11th, 15th and 21st Company, Tielen
- *Eskadron de Gidsen* (Esk G), Lombardsijde
- Bij VA Para-Cdo (ArtBttr), Brasschaat
- 20 *Bataljon Logistiek* (20 Bn Log), Herverlee
- Para Training Center (TrgC/CE), Schaffen
- Commando Training Center (TrgC/ CE), Marche-les-Dames

### Battalion Structure
The organization of the *1ste Bataljon Parachutisten* is as follows (all three airmobile infantry battalions have the same structure):
- Battalion HQ
- HQ Company with
- Company HQ
- Signal troop
- Support troop
- Electrical and mechanical engineer troop
- Medical troop*
- Recce troop

\* Medical staff is provided by the training center at Schaffen / Diest or Belgian Medical

*Since November 1989, Para Cdo Bde has been equipped with the Puch Pandur (6x6) armored vehicle, with which one company per infantry battalion is equipped. The Pandur company consists of three troops with four Pandurs each. The Pandur is armed with an MG 12.7mm or FNMAG 7.62mm, having a dismounted strength of two Minimi 5.56mm, one FNMAG, one Accuracy AW, and four FNC 7.62mm. The gear of the dismounted troops changes depending on the mission. An anti-tank-troop can be fitted with up to two Milan ATGWs.*

- Mortar troop (six 120mm mortars or six 81mm mortars depending on the mission)
- Sniper troop
- 3 infantry companies with
- HQ (1 NR493PRB 60mm mortar is issued to the company commander)
- 2 infantry companies
- 1 anti-tank troop with 6 Milan Anti-Tank Guided Weapons (ATGW)

**Vehicles and Weapons of an Infantry Company**
- 3 Bombardier Iltis (4x4)
- 17 Unimog 1350gl 2t **
- 3 MAN 11.136HA
- 6 combat boats (10 soldiers)
- 3 light recce boats
- 6 Milan ATGW
- 4 12.7mm MG
- 3 60mm mortars
- 9 FNMAG 7.62mm MG
- 9 MINIMI 5.56mm MG
- 9 Accuracy 7.62mm sniper rifles

** One company per battalion is equipped with the Pandur (6x6) wheeled troop carrier.

*A Pandur (6x6) of 16th Company, 2nd Commando Bataillon is seen during the FTX "Yellow Viper 2002." Even 16th Company consists of two infantry troops and one anti-tank troop armed with Milan. A total of 54 Pandur were delivered to the Belgian Para-Cdo Brigade: 41 APCs (Armored Personnel Carrier), 5 CPVs (Command Post Vehicle), 4 MRVs (Mechanized Recovery Vehicle) and 4 ambulance versions (with longer wheel base).*

The two gun troops of the artillery battery from Brasschaat are equipped with six 105mm LG1 Mk2 Light Guns. Weighing 1.5 tons, the gun is air droppable and has a maximum range of 17.5km (11 miles). It is towed by a Unimog 1350L. Those vehicles participated in the parade on the occasion of the national holiday in Brussels on 21 July 2002. The battery owns a further three M101A1 field guns that are no longer in service but are used for firing salutes during celebrations!

### The Parachutists Training Center

The Para Trg/CE at Schaffen/Diest is responsible for training aspiring parachutists. Three different drop courses are offered:

1. Class A: Basic training for Para Cdo Bde soldiers that includes eight drops (fully equipped with one night drop).
2. Class B: Training for Para Cdo Bde soldiers that includes four balloon drops. This course is even available for Belgian regular soldiers.
3. Class C: Six-month training course with automatic and manual canopy-opening mechanisms.

The training center consists of three companies with special tasks and training missions:

HQ with staff company:
- Radio troop
- Troop of electrical & mechanical engineers
- Field ambulance troop
- Reconnaissance troop
- Meteorological section (Air Force)

Technical company
- HQ
- Parachutists' gear troop
- Balloon troop
- Platoon electrical & mechanical engineers

Drop training company
- HQ
- Training platoon
- Support troop
- Test and evaluation troop
- Video troop

### The Commando Training Center

The Commando Training Center at Marche-les-Dames near Namur is responsible for special training (commando/battle) that is divided into two main tasks:

1. Primary training missions
- Basic training for para-commandos
- Commando courses on A and B level
- Survival training
- Physical tests
- Special courses

2. Secondary tasks and training missions:
- Para Cdo Bde's reserve for all kinds of missions
- Alpine and amphibious training

The ambulance commando recently received the new "Gator" 6x6 all-terrain vehicle manufactured by John Deere. Providing support for the Para Cdo Bde's ambulance tasks, it can be used for carrying casualties, as a command post vehicle, or simply as a transport vehicle.

- Checking special gear
- Supervision of guest nation training
- Public affairs operations (e.g., showing bivouacs and displays)

The Commando Training Center has four companies, each having special tasks:

1. Basic Training company for tactical, technical and physical training (4 months)
2. Education company
- Para-Commando education for officers and aspirants (4 months)
- Basic sniper course (6 weeks)
- Sniper instructor course (6 weeks)
- Camouflage course (1 week)

3. Camp company
- A-level commando course (4 weeks)
- B-level commando course (3 weeks)
- Commando assistant course and commando instructor course (8 weeks)
- Alpine leader course (5 weeks)
- Basic commando course (1 week)
- Survival training (1 week)

4. Staff and HQ company

The wheelbase of the Pandur (6x6) ambulance version is 0.6m (2 feet) longer than that of the APC version. The vehicle is propelled by a 6-cylinder, supercharged, diesel-fuel engine that enables it to accelerate from 0 to 50km/h (31 mph) in 15 seconds!

*The infantry battalions' weaponry is varied. Every fusilier group has one FNMAG 7.62mm that can be either used with a bipod or be mounted on a vehicle. When it is mounted, targets can be engaged up to a range of 1200m (1312 yards). Additionally, it can be fitted with a passive night sight device.*

*Snipers are trained in the infantry battalions as well. They are armed with the Accuracy G-22 7.62mm sniper rifle.*

### Missions and Training

The Para-Cdo Bde works closely with MND(C) and can operate at any time and at any place in the world within peacekeeping or out-of-area operations (e.g., Africa). Some of those operations are Operation "Restore Hope" within the scope of "UNOSOM II" in the Kismayo region of Somalia and the major evacuation operation named "Blue Beam" from September to October 1991, when some 5345 European people had to be evacuated from Rwanda and Zaire. Para-commandos also supported Operation "Green Stream," preventing locals from committing cruelties during the changeover of power in Zaire.

To enable troops to complete their missions, a large air transport capacity and modern and reliable staff and material are absolutely necessary. To meet their requirements, the Para-Cdo Bde possesses highly strategic and operative mobility, including their famous anti-tank weaponry and the capability to operate in rough conditions and in any kind of terrain.

In peacetime, the Brigade has a total of 3000 temporary and full-time soldiers. Air transport is provided by the Belgian 15th Air Transport Wing, which has a total of 11 C-130 Hercules transport aircraft divided between the 20th and 21st Smd (Squadron) from Melsbroek/Bruxelles. During airborne operations, air support is provided by the 36 F-16 jets of the two flying wings (the 2nd W Tac [Tactical Wing] at Florennes and 10th W Tac at Kleine Brogels) of the TAF (Tactical Air Force).

But it is neither just the Brigade's staff nor its organization that guarantees permanent combat preparation; the most important factor is the famous sophisticated training system. Every single soldier who decides to join the Para Cdo Bde has to pass a comprehensive physical examination at the Armed Forces Medical Center and a five-month training program at the Commando Training Center at Marche-les-Dames following one month of parachutist training at the Parachutist Training Center at Schaffen. The last and most interesting part is no doubt the night and day air drop from C-130 aircraft using weather balloons!

*Two Iltis vehicles belonging to the "pathfinders" are prepared for live firing on a range. During live firing missions, a red flag is affixed to the rear of the vehicle. A fourth soldier checks the security and reports after every shot. The soldier sitting in the back is wearing a French parka.*

The vehicle used by the recce troop's leader carries the sign "R6" on the bumper. It is fitted with a telescopic antenna mast at the rear to provide communication.

A group of fusiliers prepares for action. Every soldier of Para Cdo Bde must complete four months of basic training. Every recruit goes through a one-month basic commando course at the Commando Training Center. After being redeployed to his unit, the recruit will take more courses depending on his task.

A sniper displays his AW 7.62mm sniper rifle. The weapon is camouflaged by painting it with camouflage colors and covering the metal parts with cloth taken from old dresses.

Each infantry battalion's HQ company has one sniper troop. These snipers are fully trained. It is believed a sniper troop is composed of about nine snipers, with three trainees. Their main weapon is the Accuracy (AW) G-22 with a 6x42 telescopic sight made by Schmidt & Bender. There are no strict rules concerning their personal kit; it often depends on what gear the individual soldier wants to use. Clothes and equipment purchased from army surplus stores or borrowed from other NATO comrades can often be found. Here a well-camouflaged sniper is almost invisible after taking up a concealed position.

All Belgian Pandurs are sent to the EMI (Espace Mobile International) workshops at Aubange for final assembly. All vehicles are fitted with the Automatic Drive Terrain Management (ADM) system developed by Steyr-Puch, an air conditioner, and a GPS (Global Positioning System) device.

Soldiers dismount from the Pandur through two large rear doors. One soldier overseeing the whole procedure provides security.

The battalion commander has one Bombardier Iltis. This vehicle is equipped with a telescopic antenna mast and a BMAS radio kit. Fully equipped, the vehicle weighs about 2.2 tons.

Along with each infantry battalion's HQ company's anti-tank troop, the Para Cdo Bde has three more Bombardier Iltis vehicles fitted with Milan that are integrated into the "pathfinder" troops.

51

This Unimog 1350L (4x4) of Parachutist Training Center (TrgC Para) at Schaffen is fitted with a cab. It belongs to the meteorological section and measures all the meteorological data required for air dropping using a weather balloon, especially the wind speed at the drop zone. In 1996, the Unimog 1350 gl replaced the old 1.5-ton Unimog S404 that has performed its duty in the Para-Commando Brigade since 1965/66.

The infantry battalions´ support troops (RAV- Ravitaillering) also use the MAN 11.136 HA (4x4) that will be withdrawn in future and replaced with a new truck.

Air transport is provided by C-130 Hercules of 15th Air Transport Wing of Melsbroek/Bruxelles. At the time of writing, the Belgian Air Force owns 11 C-130 aircraft and is planning to procure 11 new A400M transport aircraft. It is noteworthy that Luxemburg has an agreement with the Belgian Air Force allowing the use of one transport aircraft for their tasks.

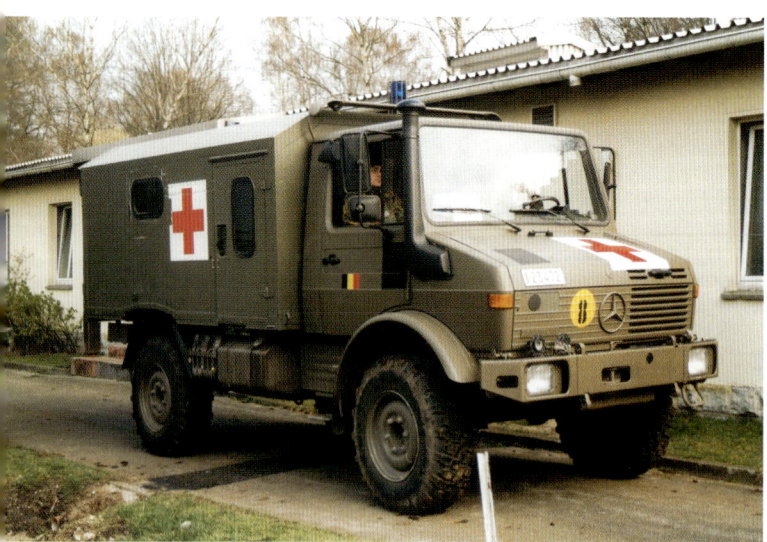

The Unimog 1350L (4x4), which is fitted with a cab, is used mostly for transporting casualties. Four reclining casualties can be carried though its cab since it is lower than the German version.

The canopies of the parachutes are folded immediately following a drop, then they are delivered to the technical company of the Trg/CE for maintenance and preparation for further action.

# The MSU
## Italian Carabinieri in the Former Yugoslavia   Alberto Scarpitta

*MSU forces are fully mobile, employing many different vehicles, as well as some armored cars and APCs. (P. Valpolini)*

### The Third Millennium Force

The Multinational Specialized Unit (MSU) was created in Bosnia in 1998, following the Dayton Agreements, to provide the Implementation/Stabilization Force with an intermediate-level instrument that was somewhere between a purely military force and the International Police Task Force . . . an unarmed civilian police force. The Multinational Specialized Unit is a police force with military status and an overall police capability. Its mandate covers the whole territory of Bosnia-Herzegovina, and it has the same rules of engagement as the military units, differing only in that it is specialized in police activities.

The MSU, which can apply the necessary force when facing a crisis situation relating to public order, disturbances and terrorist attacks, is a unit made up of Italian troops. The largest component is furnished by the Italian Carabinieri, a large police force with military status of about 112,000 men covering mainly home security operations, but also earmarked for military police duties.

MSU Carabinieri have substantial experience fighting organized crime and terrorism. They possess human resources and dedicated investigative tools to analyze the structure of subversive and criminal organizations, and they provide prevention and repression resources to be used as an SFOR asset. MSU conducts general patrolling operations in order to maintain a regular presence within the contingent area of responsibility (AOR). Such operations, which are in support of SFOR routine patrol activity, allow the MSU to interact with the local community while deepening their overall knowledge of evolving criminal and security assets of each area.

The MSU in Bosnia, which is based at Butmir near the Sarajevo airport, is a Carabinieri regimental-level unit consisting of about 540 elements. It has a regimental staff, one support company, one maneuver

company, and one operative battalion of four companies. One of these is wholly Italian, two more are Italian with a Romanian and a Slovenian platoon attached to them, and the fourth is manned by the *Gendarmeria Nacional* of Argentina. The maneuver company is composed of specialized elements of the Carabinieri from the Tuscania 1st Parachute Carabinieri Regiment (one quick reaction platoon), the GIS (two SWAT squads from the Carabinieri anti-terrorist unit), and the ROS (the *Reparto Operativo Speciale*, which furnishes about twenty detectives).

*The Italian Carabinieri became a separate service with the important role of providing personnel for NATO's Multinational Specialized Units. (P. Valpolini)*

The MSU in Bosnia-Herzegovina uses dogs to support riot-control activity. (P. Valpolini)

The MSU's primary tasks are:
- Maintenance of a secure environment
- Law enforcement
- Presence patrolling
- Information gathering operations
- Special police operations
- Counter-civil disturbance operations
- Criminal intelligence and counter-terrorism
- Crimes related to military security
- VIP escort operations.

When created, the MSU assigned a liaison officer to each SFOR divisional headquarters. The operative control of the force remained with the MSU commander. In public order operations, the competent division assumed tactical control. Later, a new concept called "Blue Box" was introduced. According to this criterion, the MSU has total responsibility for the operations in a specific area. It retains full command and control of its men and, if necessary, can also take tactical control of military units engaged in the blue box other than the Carabinieri and other MSU forces.

The MSU concept has become an important asset of NATO peacekeeping missions. Italian Carabinieri, with their double role of military personnel with military experience, can contribute to the peace and state-building process, defending the new state institutions against crime and terrorism threats.

### The Kosovo Multinational Specialized Unit

Following the Serb atrocities against the ethnic Albanian population in Kosovo and the NATO air strikes against Yugoslavia (operation "Allied Force"), the allies began Operation "Joint Guardian", the deployment of KFOR (Kosovo Force), the international peacekeeping mission in the UN-administered province, into the region. Its mandate was to provide a safe, secure environment for all people in Kosovo and to support the UN mission (UNMIK).

SFOR units can support the Multinational Specialized Unit with assets such as armored vehicles or, as in this case, medical assistance. (P. Valpolini)

Many significant changes have occurred in Kosovo since the arrival of KFOR in June 1999.

Significantly, crime continues to decrease and many policing functions that were originally carried out by KFOR units are now being undertaken by UNMIK Police, the new UN civil police force. At present, KFOR is focusing on combating organized crime and extremism is support of the UNMIK Police and providing effective security for all communities is Kosovo. It carries out this mission in an impartial way.

KFOR has also witnessed the democratic election of a new government in Kosovo. This election sent a clear message to the international community and gave hope for the future to all the inhabitants of the region. It also provided further evidence of the continuing stability that is being seen across the province. Moreover, stability is a function of the safe and secure environment KFOR continues to provide.

Part of this effort to increase stability involves a weapons amnesty that gave all Kosovars the opportunity to hand over illegal weapon without fear of prosecution. Ordinary people who were not necessarily involved in criminal activity but who still retained weapons out of a misplaced fear for their safety had the opportunity to turn in their weapons prior to the implementation of weapons regulations by the new government of Kosovo. That initiative and the subsequent application of

The Multinational Specialized Unit is a police force with military status and an overall police capability. Its mandate covers the whole territory of Bosnia-Herzegovina, and it has the same rules of engagement as the military units, differing only in that it is specialized in police activities. (P. Valpolini)

*According to the "Blue Box" operational concept, the responsibility for the operations in a specific area belongs to the MSU, which has full command and control of its men. If necessary, it can also take tactical control of military units engaged in the blue box other than the Carabinieri and other MSU forces. (P. Valpolini)*

the new legislation have contributed to the improvement in security and the reduction of violent crime. Every weapon and round of ammunition removed from circulation is one less potential tragedy and one more step toward a peaceful, tolerant society.

KFOR units were also heavily involved with the launch of the Euro currency. KFOR provided storage and security during its launch and further protection as it was moved to banks throughout Kosovo.

KFOR's primary mission has not changed. Its mandate is to maintain a military force capable of monitoring and ensuring compliance with United Nations Resolution 1244, the Military Technical Agreement and relevant international undertaking, statements and regulations, and be ready to respond promptly to any violations in order to restore compliance, using military force if necessary. KFOR accomplishes its mission through five Multinational Brigades, with contributing forces from 38 nations and about 38,000 personnel.

Soon after the arrival of the military force, it was decided to also create in Kosovo a Multinational Specialized Unit, a police force with military status just like the Bosnian MSU and with similar tasks. The creation within SFOR of a Multinational Specialized Unit with the same mandate as other SFOR elements enhanced SFOR's ability to support local authorities in responding to civil disorder (without engaging in police functions), assisting in the return of refugees and displaced persons, and installing elected officials. The unit had to be a KFOR asset, not a national one, and was to depend directly on a KFOR commander, with an overall police capability competent throughout the Kosovo area of responsibility (AOR).

The KFOR MSU is based in Pristina, near the Force Headquarters, with detachments in all sectors of the Multinational Brigades. Each detachment in the KFOR AOR has a different strength depending on the public order and security situation of the area. The total strength is about 350 police officers. The MSU's structure relies on an Italian Carabinieri regiment HQ with a supply and service platoon, a special operations company, and a military police battalion with two Carabinieri companies, each reinforced by a foreign platoon (from the French Gendarmerie and Estonian Army, respectively). The special company is composed of an elite Parachute Carabinieri platoon of the Tuscania Regiment, a small SWAT squad of the GIS (the Carabinieri anti-terrorist unit), two armored squads with armored infantry carriers, and a VIP-protection team.

*A charge is made to resolve dramatic public disorder by dispersing the crowd or limiting their offensive power. (P. Valpolini)*

*One Carabinieri company of the MSU in Bosnia-Herzegovina has a Slovenian platoon attached to it that belongs to the 17th Military Police Battalion, which is based in Lubiana. The unit has some BOV M-86 armored personnel carriers armed with the Browning M-2 heavy machine gun. The Slovenian MPs are armed with 9mm Parabellum HK MP5 A3 sub-machine guns. (P. Valpolini)*

security team to the platoon leader, and two more drivers for the platoon leader and the blocking team.

The platoon leader and the squads represent the primary intervention unit, while the blocking team is used to single out and block the most violent elements of the crowd, who are taken beyond the contact line through rapid maneuvering. The support team guarantees the security of the platoon against firebombs using extinguishers and it helps them remove obstacles (barriers, barbed wire, etc.) that could limit the platoon's movement. Two Carabinieri are put in place for the security of the platoon leader.

The Italian anti-riot platoon uses some static crowd control formations, which are basically defensive. When facing violent elements, the unit creates a **simple-line formation,** a parallel line far from the crowd to avoid contact and stay out of reach of any hurled items. The platoon leader places himself at the center of the formation along with the security team, and the squads take up position behind him. Placed behind the entire formation are the blocking team and the support team armed with extinguishers and tools for removing obstacles.

When the situation becomes more critical, the platoon creates a **double-line formation** with two parallel lines. The Carabinieri shield can cover a man entirely only if he kneels down. To protect a full line of soldiers, the first line kneels behind their shields and the second stands right behind the first line, holding their shields in front so the two shields provide a man with full coverage. The platoon leader takes his place at the center of the first line along with the security team. Two squads are positioned behind him, and the blocking team is placed behind the whole formation. At the order "*Testuggine*" (tortoise), which is given when objects are launched against the platoon, the second line covers the first line with their shields while proceeding toward the crowd, imitating the famous tactic used by the ancient Roman Legion.

When the resistance of the crowd is particularly robust and a way to pass through the crowd is needed, the platoon leader gives to order "reinforced wedge", placing himself at the head of the formation, surrounded by the squad leaders and the security team. The squads form a slanting double line, then the platoon moves slowly towards the crowd with a rhythmic step to take advantage of the threatening, coordinated movement and acoustic effects. They also beat their truncheons against their shields. If the crowd does not appear to withdraw, the MSU anti-riot platoon continues to march in step and the men raise their truncheons.

The MSU unit has the same mandate as KFOR: to enforce law and order until the UN mission can fully assume this responsibility. This is achieved through patrols, general surveillance, checkpoints, response to emergency calls, search operations, border control, investigation of criminal activities, and the arrest or detention of suspected criminals.

### The Anti-Riot Platoon

The MP companies furnish in turn the MSU-ready Anti-Riot Platoon, a specialized quick reaction unit in KFOR hands. In the theatre of operations it is an operative tool to guarantee public order in unsafe situations. It finds its enforcement in the so called "Blue Box", a delimited area where the situation concerning public order is getting worse that is made safe by the KFOR Multinational Brigades, who provide force protection and security in the surrounding area.

The Italian anti-riot platoon, which is much different from the similar tool used in national territory, is made up of 37 elements. All told, they consist of a platoon leader, four squads of five Carabinieri and a driver each, one support team, one five-man blocking team, one two-element

Photographed in Mostar, this Carabinieri Land Rover Defender 90 belongs to the Bosnia-Herzegovina MSU.

All the Carabinieri attached to the MSU belong to a mobile battalion or regiment and are normally employed in these kind of activities at football matches and political demonstrations. The not-too-young average age of the Carabinieri and their experience of being engaged in urban clashes make them a tough opponent for the violent crowd.

At the order "charge", the rhythmic step becomes a forward rush. At this particular moment it is very important to maintain a perfect front line in the forefront of the contact with the crowd in order to prevent demonstrators from penetrating the formation. The Carabinieri must quickly follow up the events to disperse the crowd and force it to stop. The charge is made to resolve a dramatic display of public disorder by disbursing the crowd or limiting its offensive power.

Night checkpoint in Kosovo. Constant territorial control improves general security. The black beret easily identifies this Italian member of the MSU as a Carabiniere belonging to a mobile battalion or regiment.

The French Gendarmerie platoon contributes to the MSU anti-riot platoon with a smaller unit composed of 18 elements: the platoon leader, one deputy platoon leader, two squads made of six Gendarmes, and one support team made of two elements supplied with a grenade launcher, and two of the platoon's drivers. The first squad is supplied with the shields, while the second is issued only long batons. The support team uses tear gas or grenades to guarantee the security of the platoon when the situation becomes worse.

The French platoon usually has a double-line formation. When the public disorder worsens, the second line puts on their helmets under protection of the shields of the first line. Then the first line dons helmets under the protection of the second line. Thus prepared, the two lines take a defensive position, the first covering themselves with the shields while the second line employs their truncheons.

### The Carabinieri 2nd Mobile Brigade

In March 2000, the Carabinieri, which were formerly part of the Army, became a separate service within the Italian Armed Forces. To support their contributions to operations abroad and their increasing involvement in out-of-area missions, the Carabinieri's General Staff created the 2nd Mobile Brigade in Livorno in September 2001. It is composed of a Brigade Headquarters, an intelligence cell, the 7th Carabinieri Regiment "*Trentino Alto Adige*" based in Laives near Bolzano, the 13th Carabinieri Regiment "*Friuli Venezia Giulia*" of Gorizia, the Tuscania 1st Parachute Carabinieri Regiment headquartered in Livorno (formerly assigned to the Army Folgore Parachute Brigade), and the *Gruppo Intervento Speciale* (G.I.S.), the Corps' anti-terrorist unit.

The Brigade's primary task is to train, equip, organize, and co-ordinate its units before being deployed abroad to operate with their specific capabilities in support of multinational forces in peacekeeping

These two Carabinieri, seen in Dakovica (Kosovo), are not assigned to the MSU but fulfill military police tasks within the multinational force.

Static portrait of a member of the Tuscania Parachute Regiment. Elements of this elite unit serve with both MSUs in the former Yugoslavia, generally with reserve roles and quick reaction force tasks. Note the red beret of the airborne troops, the special combat vest and the silenced HK MP-5 SD3 sub-machine gun fitted with a Sure Fire light.

Weapons and special equipment used by the special company of the Kosovo MSU range from a shotgun to a Leica Vector laser range-finding binocular to various night-vision devices.

missions. It furnishes a framework for the MSUs in the former Yugoslavia and about fifty percent of their strength, as these units are usually augmented by Carabinieri coming from other mobile battalions that have been tasked with riot-control missions in Italy or from the territorial organization of the Corps. These add-on Carabinieri, coming from different units, receive specific training at the Brigade's location to be able to operate together and with the same tactics before being sent abroad. To further increase this capacity, 2nd Brigade is also planning to create a specific training center where MSU units will be able to consolidate before deploying to the theatre of operations.

The Brigade units have a double role, combining the characteristics of light combat force with the possibility of being deployed at a very high level of specialization in the classic roles of the Carabinieri, such as fighting organized crime, and providing territorial security and riot control.

The 7th and 13th Regiments are comprised of headquarters, headquarters company, and a mobile battalion with a small command element, and three companies of four platoons. The headquarters company has five platoons: command, communications, maintenance, armored cars (Fiat 6616 with 20mm automatic cannon), and weapons. The elite Tuscania Regiment has a similar organization, with the further addition of a training company that selects and trains aspirants through a demanding nine-month course.

The secretive G.I.S., which is composed of between 70 and 150 operators, includes a command element, one training section, one sniper/scout section, and three operative sections, which are in turn divided into four-man teams.

The Beretta M-12 is still in wide use with the Carabinieri. This is a Model 12S, the latest model of the Beretta sub-machine gun.

*A member of the Gruppo Intervento Speciale, the anti-terrorist unit of the Corps, wears the typical assault dress, combat vest produced by the firm Radar, and fire-retardant underwear. Note the radio set for personal communication within the assault team.*

*The right side of a G.I.S. operator in full assault gear. The HK MP-5A5 sub-machine gun is fitted with a second generation EOTech Holosight, a sight involving holographic technology in which a hologram of a reticule pattern is recorded on a head-up display window. The pistol is the usual Beretta 92SB or F in use in the Corps.*

The sniper/scout section is composed of very experienced elements that are the first ones to reach the mission location in order to report to the GIS commander as much data on the target as possible. After gathering target reconnaissance, they assume typical sniper functions to support the entry teams. The section is further divided into three teams, usually assigned to the operative sections.

The training section is responsible for the selection and training process of future operators. Aspirants, all coming from the Tuscania Regiment, must have been in the service for at least four years and be younger than thirty. Following the usual physical and medical tests, they must survive a grueling 21-week basic training course, learning such skills as fast shooting, close-quarter and CT combat, forced entry, demolitions, climbing techniques, rappelling, unarmed combat, fast driving, and the use of special equipment. Each survivor is assigned to one experienced operator for further on-the-job training and go through a probationary period of service. Before becoming fully operative, the new GIS member will receive additional training within the unit and with other Carabinieri training facilities, such as the Carabinieri Alpine Training Centre of Selva di Val Gardena in the Eastern Alps.

[Editor's Note: The importance of the training provided to the Carabinieri cannot be underestimated. Deployed to such high-risk theatres of operation as the former Yugoslavia and Iraq, they face life-threatening dangers that only such highly volatile locations can offer. On 12 November 2003, 11 Carabinieri were among at least 17 Italians and nine Iraqis that were killed when a suicide bomber exploded a truck at an Italian police base in Nasiriyah in Iraq. This was Italy's highest military death toll since World War II.]

*The G.I.S. is armed with many weapons that are not used in conventional Carabinieri units. This operator displays a Steyr AUG 5.56mm assault rifle, the carbine version with a 417mm (16.4-inch) barrel and a Picatinny rail fitted with a Trijicon Acog 4x32 sight.*

When facing violent elements, the unit creates a simple-line formation, a parallel line far from the crowd, to avoid contact and thrown items. When the situation becomes more critical, the platoon creates a double-line formation with two parallel lines.

The platoon leader takes his place at the center of the first line, along with the security team. Two squads are placed behind him, and the blocking team takes up their position behind all the formation.

To protect a full line of soldiers, the first line kneels behind their shields and the second stands right behind the first line, holding their shields in front so the two shields can provide cover for a man.

The Kosovo MSU has a 22-strong Estonian Army Military Police platoon attached to it. Note the Galil 5.5mm assault rifle, the national flag insignia on the right shoulder and the KFOR armband on the left arm. The Galil is the SAR (Short Assault Rifle) version, with a shortened barrel and folding stock, without bipod and carrying handle.

The French Gendarmerie make a very professional contribution to the Kosovo MSU. Note their small shields and the specific anti-riot protection.

The French anti-riot platoon usually employs a double-line formation. When public disorder worsens, the second line puts on their helmets while protected by the shields of the first line. Then the second line performs the same favor for the first line.

The French Gendarmerie anti-riot platoon is composed of 18 elements: the platoon leader, one deputy platoon leader, two squads made up of six Gendarmes, one support team made up of two elements supplied with a grenade launcher, and two drivers.

According to the "Blue Box" concept, MSU elements take tactical control of military units engaged in operations other than Carabinieri, who are directly under the command of KFOR and have an overall police capability in the Kosovo area of responsibility. In this weapon search exercise, the soldier with the loudspeaker gives notice of the imminent house search, while two Carabinieri are ready to flank the soldiers.

Using tear gas or grenades, the support team of the French ant-riot platoon guarantees the security of the unit when the situation becomes more dangerous.

The French Spectra helmet can be fitted with a protective visor for riot-control situations. The French Gendarmerie has a specific training center for training and drilling the Corps units involved in crowd- and riot-control operations.

Army personnel and Carabinieri military policemen prepare to conduct a forced entry. The MP on the left is armed with a Beretta M-12S sub-machine gun with a Sure Fire light attached. The soldiers furnish general security but normally are not directly involved in possible arrests.

Two violent elements who have been arrested by the Carabinieri after the house search are conducted to the MSU barracks for further questioning. Many people in Kosovo are involved in oraganized crime and political extremism or still possess illegal weapons.

Sniper of the 13th Carabinieri Regiment of the 2nd Mobile Brigade. He is armed with a Heckler and Koch 7.62mm G3 SG/1 sniper rifle, which is basically the G3A3 fitted with a special trigger unit and a telescope with variable power from x1.5 to x6. The mount employed fits over the receiver and allows use of the iron sights without dismounting the telescope. The sniper also carries a 9mm Beretta Model 92 pistol in a low-ride assault holster, held secure by an adjustable elastic leg strap. Visible on the left shoulder is the microphone for the personal radio. Note the black beret bearing the badge of the Carabinieri mobile units.

Carabinieri of the 2nd Mobile Brigade use the Franchi 12-guage SPAS-15 MIL shotgun, a weapon that offers both semi-automatic and manual pump action. The SPAS-15 is considered to be well suited for police use where there is a requirement to fire specific ammunition and non-lethal cartridges of varying ballistic performance. It is fed by means of a 6-round box magazine.

Slovenian military policemen belonging to the 17th Military Police Battalion operate closely with the Italian Carabinieri within the MSU in the former Yugoslavia. The battalion, whose members wear green berets and "VP" (Slovenian version of "MP") brassards, is very active in the international theatre. It drills and prepares MP contingents that have taken part in the NATO-led peace support operation "Joint Forge" in Bosnia-Herzegovina since February 1999.

Two parachutist Carabinieri belonging to the elite Tuscania Regiment operating in Bosnia-Herzegovina. They wear army-style uniforms with the classic red beret of the airborne troops and Israeli Ephod web gear. These Carabinieri, who have the double role of soldier and policeman, possess a techno-professional store of the highest degree.

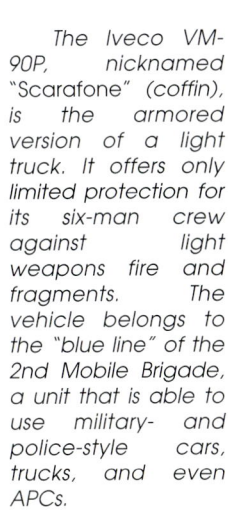

The Iveco VM-90P, nicknamed "Scarafone" (coffin), is the armored version of a light truck. It offers only limited protection for its six-man crew against light weapons fire and fragments. The vehicle belongs to the "blue line" of the 2nd Mobile Brigade, a unit that is able to use military- and police-style cars, trucks, and even APCs.

The VM-90Ps are used for light escort and liaison duties in the former Yugoslavia. This truck, which is seen at the HQ of the Italian contingent in Bosnia, is assigned to the commanding officer of the Tuscania Parachute Carabinieri Regiment.

K O S O V O

**MSU**

MULTINATIONAL SPECIALIZED UNIT

MSU Carabinieri in Mitrovia, Kosovo face down multiethnic disorder. They wear light body armor over blue police-style uniforms.

The Tuscania Parachute Carabinieri Regiment has two motorized companies with VM-90 light trucks and one mechanized company with VCC1 tracked armored personnel carriers. Called "Camillino", the VCC1 is a modified version of the American M-113 fitted with additional steel armor and a roof-mounted 12.7mm Browning heavy machine-gun in an armored position. It carries a crew of two and seven infantrymen. One of them, the crew commander, has his own cupola beside that of the machine gunner.